Out of Bounds
Out of Control

Out of Bounds
Out of Control

REGULATORY ENFORCEMENT AT THE EPA

James V. DeLong

CATO
INSTITUTE
Washington, D.C.

Library of Congress Cataloging-in-Publication Data

DeLong, James V., 1938–
  Out of bounds, out of control : regulatory enforcement at the
  EPA / James V. DeLong.
    p. cm.
  Includes bibliographical references and index.
  ISBN 1-930865-29-5 (paper : alk. paper) -- ISBN 1-930865-30-9
    (cloth : alk. paper)
  1. United States. Environmental Protection Agency. 2.
Environmental law—United States. I. Title.

KF3775.Z9 D45 2002
344.73'046--dc21

                                                          2002074012

Cover design by Amanda S. Elliott.
Cover photography © Ed Bock/The Stock Market.
Printed in the United States of America.

CATO INSTITUTE
1000 Massachusetts Ave., N.W.
Washington, D.C. 20001
www.cato.org

Contents

Introduction

In theory, enforcement occupies a specific pigeonhole in an orderly regulatory universe. Congress passes a law mandating that specified actions be carried out, or avoided, by organizations and individuals in the private sector. Substantial authority is delegated to an agency, which promulgates rules to elaborate on Congress's intent, resolve unsettled issues, and fill in legal gaps. The agency also establishes mechanisms to monitor and compel compliance—information collection systems, investigators, prosecutors, judges, rules of procedure, and penalty schedules.

If one asks how such an enforcement system is working, the questions are standard. Is it adequately funded? Are the people doing their jobs? Do regulated entities know what is required of them? Are they complying? Are the penalties imposed commensurate with our sense of justice? Is prosecutorial discretion exercised appropriately to allow for extenuating circumstances? Does the institution have a reasonable case selection process, given that it cannot pursue every violator? Are like cases treated alike? Do the institutional arrangements—such as the division of power between Washington and regional offices—foster efficiency and effectiveness? Are the enforcers corrupt, either directly or through political pressure?

These are fair questions to ask about EPA's environmental enforcement procedures, and many analysts have indeed asked them.[1] However, this list of questions is seriously incomplete, because a deeper issue, more important than any of these, is not addressed: Are the agency's enforcement procedures and activities consistent with the rule of law?

The phrase, "rule of law," is frequently used but seldom defined. F. A. Hayek provided a definition directly relevant to the analysis of EPA regulatory enforcement when he said,

> Nothing distinguishes more clearly conditions in a free country from those in a country under arbitrary government than the observance in the former of the great principles known

as the Rule of Law. Stripped of all technicalities, this means
that government in all its action is bound by rules fixed
and announced beforehand—rules which make it possible
to foresee with fair certainty how the authority will use its
coercive powers in given circumstances and to plan one's
individual affairs on the basis of this knowledge.[2]

Judged by these criteria, EPA enforcement policy most certainly
does not comport with the rule of law. The full array of environmental regulation is so detailed, obscure, and all-encompassing that no
regulated entity can possibly ascertain and maintain full compliance
with all mandates at all times. In consequence, EPA maintains broad
discretion to define what is and is not a violation of the law. It fights
vigorously to avoid any checks on this discretion. It often exercises
its discretion retroactively or arbitrarily. It makes examples of people
who dispute the agency's interpretation of its power or who express
doubts about the absolute primacy of EPA's mission, such as those
who assert the validity of economic values or who argue that tradeoffs between environmental and other values should be addressed.

EPA also blurs lines that separate legislative, executive, and adjudicatory functions. Using its vast powers to "interpret" vague statutes, it makes the laws that define its own powers, then investigates,
prosecutes, adjudicates, and penalizes. Judicial checks are weak and
sporadic. This panoply of power breeds regulatory zealotry and a
disregard for the rights of the regulated.

Such a lack of dedication to the rule of law by a government
agency is hardly a minor complaint. As Robert Conquest, the great
scholar of 20th century totalitarianism, recently emphasized,

The mere creation of democratic institutions and electoral
processes is nothing like enough to guarantee the survival
of democracy unless and until an evolution of political attitudes, and an acceptance of consensual principles, really
permeate the society in question, and above all the Rule of
Law that represents and realizes these principles.[3]

To support these harsh judgments, this analysis proceeds in four
steps: Chapter 1 is primarily descriptive. It describes EPA's scope
of authority, the universe of regulated entities, and the enforcement
mechanisms that the agency brings to bear. It contains basic numbers
on the enforcement activities—cases brought and concluded, money

collected, matters referred to the Department of Justice. It examines the number of entities with which EPA must deal and provides basic data on the numbers and types of cases it processes.

Chapter 1 also makes a serious substantive point. While EPA public relations materials convey the image of an agency under siege, continually fighting recalcitrant industry, the agency's own data create a rather different picture. In reality, compliance with the environmental laws by U.S. business appears to be quite good. The agency has to scramble to keep up its flow of enforcement cases, and most of its work involves not-very-significant violations of paperwork requirements or minor releases of pollutants. The agency's shrill assaults on the regulated community are not justified by the information available on the actual extent of that community's transgressions.

Chapters 2 through 7 provide a bill of particulars on EPA's disregard for the rule of law. Those sections do not purport to be encyclopedic. They focus on a few areas that are particularly apt for purposes of illustrating what is wrong with the agency's enforcement procedures and activities. The common thread throughout this discussion is that the agency's approach to the rule of law goes beyond indifference; the EPA is actively hostile to it.

Chapter 2 considers the arbitrary nature of EPA enforcement practices. It finds that strict compliance with EPA regulations is extremely difficult and in many cases absolutely impossible. EPA is thus in a position to take action against virtually any regulated entity it chooses to attack. Moreover, the agency has total discretion over whether to treat a particular offense as a serious criminal case, a minor administrative matter, or something in between. Enforcement activities are thus inevitably arbitrary, and this arbitrariness not only violates the rule of law but actually undermines environmental protection.

Chapter 3 discusses EPA's refusal to consider whether the targets of its enforcement activities actually intended to break the law. Although there are good reasons for the law to disregard intent in some cases, those reasons do not apply in environmental enforcement. The idea that a defendant should not be convicted of a criminal offense or assessed civil penalties if he could not, with reasonable diligence, figure out what the law required is fundamental to a civil society.

Chapter 4 examines the vague and inscrutable nature of many of the regulations imposed on industry. EPA frequently changes and revises its interpretation of those regulations without providing due notice to the regulated community that changes have been or will be made. This lack of fair warning often results in prosecutions for offenses that were not obviously illegal at the time.

Chapter 5 considers how changes in regulatory standards are promulgated through the enforcement process itself. EPA frequently "clarifies" its interpretation of rules in the course of prosecution, and these clarifications are often of a sweeping nature. The agency's use of the enforcement process to make and revise laws and regulations also short-circuits the normal requirements of the rulemaking process and subverts the compromises that Congress struck between environmental protection and economic benefits. Examples of such actions include the "New Source Review" controversy concerning electric power plants, and EPA actions against the automobile industry and the diesel engine industry, all of which are reviewed briefly.

Chapter 6 continues in the same vein with an examination of how EPA, by changing the standard of evidence for what constitutes a violation of emissions regulations, effectively changes the law itself during its prosecution of cases. The so-called "Credible Evidence Rule" is a classic example of retroactive rulemaking.

Chapter 7 considers how EPA takes advantage of the vague language of environmental statutes and interprets them in such a way as to massively expand the intended scope of its operations. In effect, EPA has created entire programs out of thin air through its enforcement practices by creatively defining the language of the law. A leading example is the EPA and Army Corps of Engineers creation of the program of wetlands protection under the Clean Water Act.

Chapter 8 examines the tension created by the bifurcation of enforcement authority between the EPA and state governments. This bifurcated responsibility has encouraged partisan grandstanding, double jeopardy, and confusion in the regulated community. It has also stymied reasonable state attempts to limit the counterproductive zealotry of federal enforcement practices.

Chapter 9 reviews other civil liberties that are routinely disregarded by EPA in the course of its enforcement work. Warrantless searches and seizures, forced self-incrimination, and extortion of witnesses are common practices by environmental forces.

Chapter 10 explores various proposals for reform. Incremental reforms, proposed and occasionally adopted over the past 25 years, have accomplished little and ignore the fundamental problem: The agency has wide discretion and is not being adequately policed by the White House, the Congress, the courts, or the press. A return to the nondelegation doctrine is thus warranted. In the meantime, substituting civil for criminal charges for most violations, returning standard civil rights for defendants of agency prosecutions, and devolving enforcement to the states would be positive first steps.

1. The ABCs of Enforcement

Understanding EPA's enforcement practices must start with a survey of the agency's regulatory mission. As shown in Table 1-1, EPA administers a host of major and minor environmental statutes.

These laws are implemented by Title 40 of the *Code of Federal Regulations*, which contains 27 volumes and more than 20,000 pages. And this covers only the formal rules; further elaborations are provided by an ocean of administrative and judicial adjudications, formal guidance documents, informal letters and opinions, and interpretations delivered via meeting, telephone, e-mail, or hotline. For example, as noted in Chapter 5, EPA's explications of the requirements governing "New Source Review," which is one subprogram of a single program under the Clean Air Act, take up almost 4,000 pages.

This body of regulation applies to private entities of every type, conducting every possible type of activity. As shown in Table 1-2, EPA estimates that it deals with 1.4 million "core" facilities and 6.5 million "other" facilities, divided as indicated.

For some areas, EPA does not estimate how many entities it deals with. To do this for wetlands, for example, would require including every landowner in the United States, all of whom are actual or potential regulatees. The same would hold if lead paint, radon, used oil, or pesticides were included in the table. So even the large numbers shown in Table 1-2 do not provide a complete depiction of EPA's scope of activity.

Enforcement Philosophy: A Tale of Two Models

Such a diverse universe presents a challenge for any organization. Perhaps the most important initial decision in dealing with this challenge is what basic enforcement philosophy to adopt.

Two approaches exist—the compliance model and the law enforcement model.[1]

1

Table 1-1
EPA'S REGULATORY UNIVERSE

Statute (excluding subsequent amendments)	Date Enacted
Federal Food, Drug, and Cosmetic Act	1938
Federal Insecticide, Fungicide, and Rodenticide Act	1947
Federal Water Pollution Control Act (also known as the Clean Water Act)	1948
Clean Air Act	1955
Shoreline Erosion Protection Act	1965
Solid Waste Disposal Act	1965
National Environmental Policy Act	1970
Pollution Prevention Packaging Act	1970
Resource Conservation and Recovery Act	1970
Lead-Based Paint Poisoning Prevention Act	1971
Coastal Zone Management Act	1972
Marine Protection, Research, and Sanctuaries Act	1972
Ocean Dumping Act	1972
Endangered Species Act	1973
Safe Drinking Water Act	1974
Shoreline Erosion Control Demonstration Act	1974
Hazardous Materials Transportation Act	1975
Resource Conservation and Recovery Act	1976
Toxic Substances Control Act	1976
Surface Mining Control and Reclamation Act	1977
Uranium Mill-Tailings Radiation Control Act	1978
Asbestos School Hazard Detection and Control Act	1980
Comprehensive Environmental Response, Compensation, and Liability Act	1980
Nuclear Waste Policy Act	1982
Asbestos School Hazard Abatement Act	1984
Asbestos Hazard Emergency Response Act	1986
Emergency Planning and Community Right-to-Know Act	1986
Indoor Radon Abatement Act	1988
Lead Contamination Control Act	1988
Medical Waste Tracking Act	1988
Ocean Dumping Ban Act	1988
Shore Protection Act	1988
National Environmental Education Act	1990

SOURCE: www.epa.gov/epahome/lawintro.htm#carrying.

Table 1-2

Statute	Program	No./ Core	No./ Other
CAA	Stationary Sources	39,961	
	Mobile Sources		360,585
	Asbestos Demolition	.	94,885
	Dry Cleaners		33,863
CWA	NPDES	89,455	
	Pretreatment	30,000	
	Stormwater		200,000
	CAFOs/AFOs		6,600/?
	Wetlands		—
FIFRA	Producers/Registrants	16,124	
	Farms/Applicators		3,080,740
RCRA	Hazardous Waste Management	429,080	
	Underground Storage Tanks		969,652
SDWA	Drinking Water Systems	173,272	
	Underground Injection Wells	405,657	
TSCA	Core TSCA	183,000	
	Asbestos		1,300,000
	PCBs		500,230
Total		1,366,549	6,546,555

SOURCE: EPA, OECA, *FY98 Accomplishments Report*, EPA 200-R-99-003, June 1999, p. 10.

The compliance model takes a tolerant view of the world. It assumes that people are basically honest and decent, and want to comply with the law. Granted, a few bad actors exist, and the mailed fist must be kept in reserve to deal with them, but for the most part the job of agency enforcers is to help the regulated community comply with the rules. The compliance model recognizes that environmental laws are manifestations of a profound change in social attitudes about the environment and its protection. Pollution has declined steadily over the long term because society has grown richer and more able to afford the amenity of environmental protection, and trend lines show surprisingly little difference after the creation of

EPA.[2] Affluence changes social mores. People value a clean environment and, as more urgent needs are met, they turn more money and attention to achieving it.

The shift in social mores has a profound impact on environmental compliance. Few industries object strongly when told that new technologies must be cleaner than old or that society demands greater investment in pollution control. In part, this acceptance is due to their calculations of advantage. Tougher requirements on new plants act as barriers to entry, which improve the competitive position of existing companies.[3] But this is not the entire story. Business owners and managers live in their communities, and they act from personal beliefs and social pressures as well as purely economic incentives. Pressure has come from their shareholders, communities, and employees, and most are ready to acquiesce as long as they can be assured that their competitors are similarly situated, the rules are clear, and the requirements are likely to produce a reasonable payoff in terms of environmental improvement.[4] A compliance philosophy posits that the role of the agency should be to facilitate this broad social movement, using the heavy artillery of criminal and civil penalties only reluctantly and when necessary to bring along laggards and those who want a free ride on the compliance of others.

Part of EPA seems to follow a compliance philosophy. It generates volumes of compliance material. It publishes handbooks on industry sectors and Web pages chock full of information, and is aggressive in getting material onto the Internet. It has hotlines and help lines by the dozen. It releases a stream of press releases on agency-industry cooperation. These outreach efforts are quantified in Table 1-3.

These education efforts are real, important, and welcome. Nonetheless, EPA is dominated by a different model, one based on the stick rather than the carrot, and on harsh penalties rather than assistance with compliance. This law enforcement model is based on dark premises. It regards the private sector as a collection of profit maximizers who will seize any opportunity to break the rules. In this world, expressions of desire to comply are usually frauds, designed to lull naive regulators into dropping their vigilance. Reporting violations are not the result of human error, but deliberate attempts to mislead, gross sloppiness, or disregard for regulatory requirements. Failure of a business to devote boundless resources to complying with every EPA regulation, no matter how minor, is

Table 1-3
EPA COMPLIANCE ASSISTANCE ACTIVITIES

Telephone Hotlines:	
No. of Entities Reached	39,510
Workshops/Meetings/Training	
No. of Activities	529
No. of Entities Reached	27,026
Tools	
Developed In-House (No. of Activities)	2,285
Distributed (No. of Entities Reached)	177,382
On-Site Visits (No. of Entities Reached)	2,684

SOURCE: EPA, OECA, *FY98 Accomplishments Report*, EPA 200-R-99-003, June 1999, p. 16.

evidence of moral turpitude, as is any failure to give absolute priority to all environmental concerns, however small, over all concerns of efficiency, productivity, and cost, however large.

Even honest and expensive efforts at compliance will be penalized rather than praised if they fail to meet every jot and tittle of EPA paperwork requirements. Precision Plating in Akron, Ohio, for instance, is a 47-year-old company with two employees, engaged in the business of chrome plating. In 1997 it installed pollution control equipment at a cost of $50,000. However, the company relied on the installer to inform it of the regulatory requirements, and failed to obtain the proper inspections and permits. As a result, two things happened. A local newspaper reported that Precision was releasing chromium, which was not true, but the story cost the company about 70 percent of its business. In addition, EPA fined the company $108,000 (later reduced to $30,000) for the paperwork delinquency, even though no actual pollution had occurred. Precision paid the fine by tapping cash reserves set aside to pay for additional pollution control equipment.[5]

No matter what EPA says about "partnerships" or aid to small business, or its resolve to work with small business, the Precision Plating story seems to represent the basic mindset of the agency. Compliance activities are subordinated to the enforcement enterprise and the need to collect scalps. They are not designed to provide feedback to the agency on how it can modify its requirements so as to make compliance easier, or to develop information on areas in which the agency's requirements might impose burdens on the private sector that outweigh any environmental benefit, or to identify those areas in which the agency has failed to communicate its requirements clearly enough. The fact that Precision Plating did not know the paperwork requirements, despite good faith efforts to comply with the law, is EPA's failure, not the company's, but that is not how EPA sees the matter.

In August 2000, a maker of wire mesh in Massachusetts won a judgment against EPA under the law that allows exonerated defendants to collect legal fees from the government if a criminal prosecution is frivolous, vexatious, or in bad faith.[6] The trial judge found that the government indicted the company even though it not only lacked evidence justifying prosecution but also had failed to reveal evidence showing that the company was in fact not violating the Clean Water Act. A defense expert testified that lab test results were altered and passing scores changed to results indicating a violation.

These, and other stories, are the logical outcomes of an agency approach that emphasizes "successful" enforcement activities—in terms of indictments, prosecutions, plea-bargains, and penalties—rather than actual improvement in the environment. "Repeatedly, EPA has equated successful enforcement and enhanced environmental protection with its arithmetic success in tallying more indictments, more resolved cases, and more and more imposed penalties."[7]

The Enforcement Toolkit

EPA employs a variety of tools to monitor compliance:[8]

- The first step in EPA's enforcement ladder is the inspection. In FY98, EPA conducted 23,000 inspections at the regional level, either on its own initiative or in response to complaints from the public or workers. Some violations are taken care of informally at this level.
- The next escalation is to commence an "investigation," but the agency has only recently begun to track investigations separately, and numbers are not available.
- Informal enforcement actions can be taken. Again, the agency has not tracked investigations systematically. However, it does record that in FY98, Region II (of EPA's 10 regions) took the

following informal actions:

—Clean Air Act (CAA): 8 notices of violation and 124 notices of deficiency

—Clean Water Act (CWA): 187 warning letters

—Toxic Substances Contral Act (TSCA): 91 noncompliance notices

—Federal Insecticide, Fungicide, and Rodenticide Act (FIFRA): 1 stop order, 2 warning letters

—Resource Conservation and Recovery Act (RCRA): 90 warning letters

• With or without prior informal action, the agency can escalate a matter into a formal EPA administrative proceeding. Most statutes put a cap on the total penalty that can be imposed in an internal administrative proceeding. If the agency wants to seek more penalties, it must ask for civil enforcement in court.

• The next step, when a penalty in excess of the cap is desired, is to refer a violation to the Department of Justice for civil enforcement.

Running parallel to this system is the system of state enforcement. Many of the environmental statutes—particularly the Clean Air Act, the Clean Water Act, and the Resource Conservation and Recovery Act—are administered primarily by state environmental protection agencies, and the number of state actions substantially exceeds those initiated by EPA—11,260 to 3,381 in FY97. States also engage in constant informal enforcement, of course, but no numerical estimates of this activity exist.

Using this system, EPA issues compliance orders. It also collects money and requires regulatory targets to spend money. Collecting money means penalties—criminal or civil. Requirements that companies spend money are imposed through injunctions mandating cleanups or preventive measures or by means of settlements in which companies agree to fund Special Environmental Projects (SEPs). These are defined as "environmentally beneficial projects that may be proposed by a violator during . . . settlement . . . [its] cash penalty may be lowered if [it] chooses to perform an acceptable SEP."[9] From FY96 to FY98, 20 percent of all judicial and administrative penalty orders included a SEP. In FY98, 14 percent of orders included 221 SEPs worth $107.9 million. EPA's financial returns from its enforcement activities in FY98 are shown in Table 1-4.

Table 1-4
FINANCIAL PENALTIES

Type	Value (millions)
Criminal Penalties	$ 92.8
Civil Judicial Penalties	63.5
Administrative Penalties	28.3
Value of Injunctive Relief	1,976.7
Value of SEPs	107.9

SOURCE: EPA, OECA, *FY98 Accomplishments Report*, EPA 200-R-99-003, June 1999, p. 16.

Table 1-5
FORMAL ACTIONS DIVIDED BY STATUE FOR FISCAL YEAR 1998

	EPA			State	
Statute	Admin. Actions Initiated	Civil Refer. to DOJ	Crim. Refer. to DOJ	State Admin. Action	State Jud. Refer.
CAA	499	113		2,410	146
CWA/SDWA	1,590	96		6,960	146
RCRA	398	49		727	60
CERCLA	234	138			
FIFRA	205	4		1,163	
TSCA	218	0			
EPCRA	237	11			
TOTAL	3,381	411	266	11,260	352

SOURCE: EPA, Office of Enforcement and Compliance Assurance, *Enforcement and Compliance Assurance: FY98 Accomplishments Report*, EPA 200-R-99-003 (June 1999), pp. 94–95 (data taken from Exhibits A-4, A-5, A6).

NOTE: Criminal Referrals to the Dept. of Justice are not broken down by statute in the report.

The agency is not bound to follow only one track. It can seek both civil and criminal penalties, or it can gather evidence through a civil proceeding and then convert it into a criminal one. A whole legal literature on "parallel proceedings" exists, and analysts argue that these became more common during the Clinton administration.[10]

EPA keeps track of formal actions, both its own and those initiated by states. Table 1-5 shows the formal actions taken, divided by

Table 1-6
ACTIONS BY STATUTE AND TYPE

Statute	Compliance Orders	Penalty Order Complaints	Penalty Settlements
CAA	277	156	127
CERCLA	233	1	3
CWA	849	389	324
EPCRA	4	233	259
FIFRA	18	187	173
RCRA	49	155	149
SDWA	287	65	43
TSCA	4	214	167
TOTAL	1,721	1,400	1,245

SOURCE: EPA, OECA, *FY98 Accomplishments Report*, EPA 200-R-99-003, June 1999, pp. 90–9.

statute, for FY98. Administrative actions, which can be further divided, are shown in Table 1-6.

How Widespread Is Noncompliance?

The enforcement mindset—the assumption that businesses are constantly trying to dodge regulatory edicts—shows up in EPA's conclusions about the state of compliance with environmental law. EPA officials think that a substantial number of facilities within its jurisdiction are "in significant noncompliance" (abbreviated in EPA documents as "SNC") with requirements. EPA estimates that

- Twenty-seven percent of major National Pollution Discharge Elimination System (NPDES) sources were SNC during at least one-quarter of FY98, and another 27 percent were in a less severe category of "reportable noncompliance." (Twenty-seven percent equals 24,152 industrial sources of pollutants.)
- One-quarter of drinking water sources (43,318) are not in compliance with regard to public health standards.
- One-fifth of hazardous waste combustors and land disposal facilities are SNC.

In addition, EPA officials think this noncompliance is not limited to minor players. On the basis of inspections, the agency calculates

9

Table 1-7
SNC

Industry	No. Fac.	% SNC Air	% SNC Water	% SNC RCRA
Automotive Assembly	58	11.8	0	1.7
Iron & Steel Mills				
Integrated	23	72.7	39.1	30.4
Mini	91	21.2	2.7	4.5
Nonferrous Metals				
Aluminum Smelting & Refining	23	26.1	4.3	4.3
Copper Smelting & Refining	14	27.3	12.5	9.1
Petroleum Refining	179	45.0	11.8	14.1
Pulp Manufacturing	244	19.0	4.7	0

SOURCE: EPA, Office of Enforcement and Compliance Assurance, *Enforcement and Compliance Assurance: FY98 Accomplishments Report*, EPA 200-R-99-003 (June 1999), p. 9.

that SNC rates as of June 1998 for some major industrial facilities are as shown in Table 1-7.

It is easy to find anecdotal support for EPA's dark view of business compliance reading the press releases that come out of the agency. For example, on July 29, 1999, the agency reported that a jury had convicted a Texas company for selling pesticides to Native American Head Start programs to use in sanitizing toothbrushes. One hundred children developed problems, including mouth burns and blisters. The name of the company was Friendly Systems, Inc.[11]

In another recent case, a service station operator closed his station and walked away, leaving gasoline in the tanks and piping. Ten thousand gallons of gasoline leaked into an aquifer used by nearby residents as a source of drinking water. The operator then refused to obey orders to clean up the pollution.[12]

Cases like these could make anyone dour about the morals of the commercial world, and a steady stream of actions is directed against business owners who contract with cut-rate no-questions-asked firms for services such as disposing of hazardous waste, importing endangered species, or supplying ozone-depleting chemicals.

However, these examples need to be read with caution because, as is detailed later, the realities of cases do not always bear out the publicity of the press releases. EPA loves the ink of the initial hype, but when targets are acquitted or convicted of only minor offenses, the agency issues no press release. Nor do the agency's losses and retreats appear in the descriptions of enforcement accomplishments in its annual reports.

Nonetheless, there are real offenders out there, and real cases that need to be brought. But the key question is: What is the mix between major violations—those representing significant releases of pollutants—and those involving no actual harm to the environment, such as violations of reporting requirements, paperwork errors, or minor exceedances of existing pollution standards? Answering this question by examining EPA data is difficult, but there is good reason to believe that the number of hard offenders—those that have actually endangered public health or environmental amenities—is limited.

An initial difficulty is the lack of clarity of the term "SNC." EPA does not provide a definition in its "Enforcement Accomplishments Report." The term is defined independently by enforcement officials within each division. Noncompliance can be classified as "significant" even if it involves no release of significant amounts of pollutants. The NPDES program, for example, includes violations of reporting requirements in its definition of SNC.[13]

Second, assertions that particular industries are noncompliant cannot be taken at face value. The high estimates of the number of petroleum refineries and steel mills that are considered SNC by EPA, for instance, reflect an ongoing legal dispute over the meaning of New Source Pollution Standards, a point returned to later in this study. Here, EPA assumes that its interpretation of the law will prevail and that those who disagree are, therefore, automatically SNC. The dispute is not reflected in Table 1-6, in which the data imply that large numbers of major industries are simply ignoring environmental law.

On balance, the data in Table 1-7 appear to be, at most, a worst-case characterization. It is the most expansive definition of noncompliance.

Other EPA reports provide similarly inscrutable information. EPA reports that the agency entered into 3,479 settlements in FY98.[14] Of these, 46 percent required violators to change the way they manage their facilities *or* to reduce emissions or discharges into the environment, "while another 54 percent required violators to improve environmental management systems, take preventive action to avoid future non-compliance, or enhance the public's right-to-know."[15] This description is internally contradictory, given that management changes appear in both percentages. It is also noteworthy that more than half of the cases involved *no* releases of polluting substances. In fact, EPA's statement leaves open the possibility that *none* of those settlements involved such releases, that all required only precautionary management changes.

The same report contains an odd characterization of the results of criminal cases. It notes that "of the criminal investigations/cases concluded in FY1998 that reported an environmental benefit, the most frequently reported benefit was human health protection (28 percent), followed by ecosystem protection (18 percent)."[16] This deft phrasing raises some serious questions. What percentage of cases reported an environmental benefit? Are EPA and the Department of Justice (DOJ) in the habit of bringing cases that do *not* produce an environmental benefit? (Apparently so.) And of those that did not report an environmental benefit (a full 54 percent), exactly what kind of benefit did they report?

Another chart in the EPA 1998 enforcement report tends to confirm the suspicion that the percentage of hard violations is quite small. It shows the types of actions required in 3,103 civil settlements. Only 10 percent required a change in emissions or discharges, which strongly suggests that relatively few violations have any visible impact on the environment. Table 1-8 provides data on the types of compliance activity for civil cases in FY98.

Further support for the belief that the level of serious noncompliance is low is contained in a recent study conducted jointly by EPA and the Chemical Manufacturers Association (CMA).[17] A survey was mailed to the 50 CMA member facilities that had been party to 79 civil or administrative actions between 1990 and 1995. Of these, 27 facilities involved in 47 actions encompassing 69 "noncompliance events" returned the survey. It should be noted that the results are not a random sample of the enforcement universe. CMA is a special population, and facilities self-selected whether to participate. Table 1-9 provides an interesting picture of the types of violations and the percentages of noncompliance events.

12

Table 1-8
TYPES OF COMPLIANCE ACTIVITY: FISCAL YEAR 1998 CIVIL CASES

Activity	%	Activity	%
Reporting	25	Storage/Disposal Change	9
Monitoring/Sampling	25	Training	8
Recordkeeping	22	Permit Application	7
Remediation/Restoration	13	Industrial Process Change	5
Emissions/Discharge Change	10	Use Reduction	3
Removal	10	Remedial Design/Action	2

SOURCE: EPA, Office of Enforcement and Compliance Assurance, *Enforcement and Compliance Assurance: FY98 Accomplishments Report*, EPA 200-R-99-003 (June 1999), p. 2. Note—many cases required more than one form of compliance activity so the figures do not add up to 100%.

As Table 1-9 shows, only 16 percent of the noncompliance events (exceedances plus spills and/or releases) involved the release of excessive amounts of pollutants into the environment.

How Serious Is Noncompliance?

Yet another aspect of enforcement is the seriousness, or lack thereof, of noncompliance with regulations. Such information is provided by the narratives in EPA's annual *Enforcement and Compliance Assurance Accomplishments Report*. These reports contain the data on numbers of cases, such as the data given in the preceding tables.

The narratives cover only a small sample of the enforcement universe. The report for FY97, for example, contains descriptions of 203 non-Superfund cases brought by EPA regional offices, 5 brought by the EPA's Office of Regulatory Enforcement, 34 criminal cases filed by the DOJ, and 18 matters dealing with federal facilities. This is not a large slice of the 3,000-plus enforcement matters settled during the year, so it seems fair to assume that the matters described in the *Enforcement Accomplishments Report* represent the most significant cases pursued by EPA. Common experience indicates that government offices, called on to justify their existence and budget, will cite their most striking achievements. Yet the accounts in the *Enforcement Accomplishments Report* are surprisingly mundane. For example, in 1998, Region V (chosen at random) reported the following 15 non-Superfund-related matters:

Table 1-9
TYPES OF VIOLATIONS

Type of Violation	% of Non-compliance Events	Type of Violation	% of Non-compliance Events
Report Submissions and Reporting	29	Monitoring/Detection/Control	6
Exceedance	10	Failure to Respond	4
Operations and Maintenance	10	Labeling	3
Record Keeping	10	Equipment/Unit Design	3
Waste Identification	6	Corrective Action Activities	1
Unpermitted/Unauthorized Activity	6	Legal Agreement	0
Testing	6	Training/Certification	0
Spills/Releases	6		

SOURCE: Environmental Protection Agency/Chemical Manufacturers Association, EPA/CMA Root Cause Analysis Pilot Project: An Industry Survey (June 1999) (found at http://es.epa.gov/oeca/ccsmd/rootcause), p. 11.

- A steel company violated air permits and hazardous air pollutant standards. It agreed to a $1.25 million civil penalty and to a $1.8 million SEP.
- An oil company was charged with violating the benzene hazardous air pollutant standard. It agreed to a $678,000 civil penalty and to install a control device at a cost of $8 million.
- A poultry company was charged with causing a public water treatment plant to violate its ammonia discharge limits. The company agreed to a $501,000 penalty and SEPs costing at least $300,000.
- A quarry company expanded, and thus exceeded its load limits for dissolved oxygen and solids in water. An administrative order was issued, but the terms were not contained in the report.
- B.P. Chemicals did not notify the government of a reportable release for 13 hours, and failed to provide a written report as soon as possible. The company agreed to a SEP, installing three emergency warning sirens around the facility.
- A company failed to timely file paperwork under the Emergency Planning and Community Right-to-Know Act (EPCRA). It agreed to a SEP reducing the use and release of 120,900 pounds of toxic chemicals per year.
- Another company failed to timely file paperwork under EPCRA. It agreed to a SEP reducing the use and release of 126,200 pounds of toxic chemicals per year.
- 3M was ordered to stop selling unregistered kitchen cleaning products with pesticidal claims such as "Kills Germs!," to pay $238,000, and to spend $300,000 on corrective advertising.
- EKCO Housewares also had to stop making pesticidal claims and pay a $100,000 penalty.
- A company violated standards for burning hazardous waste in an industrial boiler in some manner that is not entirely clear. It paid a $69,400 penalty and agreed to a SEP to recapture cement kiln dust.
- A company was charged with multiple failures to supply data and to monitor its hazardous-waste burning operation, and agreed to a penalty of $400,000.
- Two persons were ordered to plug up an injection well and pay penalties of $125,800.
- A company agreed to a $48,450 civil penalty for late submission of TSCA inventory reports for 41 chemicals.

- A can company entered a consent decree for storing solvent hazardous wastes when it was not permitted to do so, and for violations of EPCRA in that it did not report information about several chemicals in use on the property. It paid a $400,000 civil penalty.
- A paint company was charged with violating the CAA, CWA, RCRA, and EPCRA, in a manner that was not specified. A consent order imposed a $4.7 million civil penalty, facility-wide corrective action, and two SEPs with a value of $1.1 million.

Although the descriptions of the cases supplied by EPA are not detailed enough to support definite conclusions, they certainly do not indicate that serious environmental harm was caused or threatened to any significant degree. Most of the cases seem to involve paperwork violations or minor releases of pollutants. Even the paint company case, which involved the most serious penalty, seems to have involved on-site contamination that posed no serious threat to human health or to the environment outside of the plant lines.

Cases reported by the other regions do not seem significantly different. Assuming that these cases were the regional offices' worst-case scenarios, one must conclude that the national dedication to protection of the environment is high and that the level of illegal releases of pollutants is low. This assumption does not necessarily contradict EPA's assertion of high levels of noncompliance with laws that are extraordinarily confusing and include many requirements of reporting and management that are not correlated with releases of pollutants. But it does raise questions about the seriousness of the infractions.

Conclusion

On the basis of EPA's own reports, it would seem that very few regulated entities violate federally imposed emissions limits and that EPA must work hard to find serious violations. This conclusion does not comport with EPA's press releases or its estimates of the percentage of facilities in "significant noncompliance," which convey an image of a lawless world in which environmental violations are rife. It does comport with the observation of environmental journalist Gregg Easterbrook that "the conventional wisdom is correct—enforcement is down. But for good reason: Pollution is declining. At the same time that enforcement numbers have fallen, virtually every U.S. environmental indicator has improved."[18]

In fact, these varying depictions can be reconciled: Regulatory compliance can be both high and low. The number of major violations—those involving more than trivial exceedances of standards or serious threats of emissions—is quite small, unless EPA's investigators are amazingly inept. On the other hand, the number of overall violations may be quite high, because EPA has developed a new wrinkle on Hayek's concern about the rule of law by creating an enforcement system that maximizes the number of violations that can be discovered and punished by the agency.

The bill of particulars on this point contains four clauses:

- The number of environmental requirements has grown so large and the level of uncertainty attached to them so great that no one can be in compliance all of the time.
- EPA and DOJ oppose any requirement that obliges the government to demonstrate that a violation was intentional or that the defendant was given fair notice of the regulatory requirements.
- EPA uses the enforcement process to interpret its laws and regulations.
- EPA has debased the standard of proof required to establish a violation.

The next several chapters explore these issues.

2. EPA Enforcement: Arbitrary and Capricious

All environmental experts attest that the number of environmental requirements is so large and the level of uncertainty attached to them so great that no one can be in compliance all of the time. As David Riesel, author of a leading legal treatise on environmental enforcement, puts it,

> The scary aspect about environmental enforcement is that few institutions can be assured they are in compliance at any specific point in time. Thus, at any one time there may be an unpermitted vent, the improper storage of hazardous wastes, an SPDES [State Pollutant Discharge Elimination System] exceedance, or a recordkeeping "glitch." These routine vagaries from the theoretical standard seldom produce harsh enforcement results unless there is another stimulus, and therein lies the problem. The stimulus may be an inspector upset over rude treatment, an accidental spill with public attention, or an on-site job injury, or disgruntled employee drawing attention to passed-over upgrade requests. Thus, regulated institutions are always at risk.[1]

Prosecutorial Discretion or Prosecutorial Whim?

Once EPA is "stimulated" to pay attention—to use Riesel's term—it has total discretion over the intensity with which it pursues a violation. For this reason, intent has become inconsequential, or even totally irrelevant, to the definition of environmental offenses. The same evidence can support informal negotiation, administrative penalties, judicially imposed civil penalties, or criminal prosecution. EPA can choose any level of action, from a verbal warning to full criminal indictment, on the basis of the same set of facts.[2]

Riesel explains government decisions to proceed criminally instead of civilly in the following terms:

Many permit holders regularly exceed some permit param-
eter. . . . Most agencies treat innocuous exceedances as civil
administrative matters, as they should. Nevertheless, the
apparent corporate indifference to the ongoing problems, a
perception that the discharger is attempting to cover up the
violations, or even a perceived disrespect for environmental
values (often meaning a lack of respect for environmental
investigators), can change that reasonable agency attitude.
The monumental difference between paying a fine in the
context of civil litigation and going to jail is the consequence
of subjective perceptions of government employees.[3]

EPA can point to internal guidance documents instructing its staff
on making the relevant distinctions. These documents incorporate
the factors a reasonable person would expect to find. A directive in
The Exercise of Investigative Discretion, for instance, emphasizes that
significant environmental harm and culpable conduct are the crucial
factors.[4] Ostensibly, these words seem to impose on the government
a requirement to charge criminal conduct only when real intent
exists and real knowledge that the environmental laws are being
violated—a requirement that has been largely interpreted out of the
formal statutory requirements (as is discussed in the next chapter).
This directive, however, is less constraining than it might seem for
three reasons:

- The directive quickly expands the meaning of the crucial terms.
  "Harm" includes not just an illegal discharge or emission but
  the *threat* of significant harm, as demonstrated by either an
  actual or *threatened* release. Furthermore, the "harm" test is
  satisfied by a failure to report a release or by illegal conduct that
  represents "a trend or common attitude within the regulated
  community." "Culpable conduct" can also be established by a
  number of factors: a history of violations, deliberate misconduct,
  concealment, tampering with monitoring devices, or failure to
  obtain required permits or documentation. In most cases, a
  prosecutor can easily find one of these expansionary conditions
  if he is inclined to look for it.
- Guidance is not binding on the agency or the prosecutors.
- Once the government decides that culpability factors are present, the actual prosecution proceeds under a lighter burden of
  proof, one not requiring proof of intent or knowledge. So the

20

prosecutor's judgment that aggravating factors existed is never put to a test in court.

Consequently, environmental lawyers do not regard the guidance as providing significant protection. For example, Riesel identifies some of the factors that tend to convert a civil matter into a criminal one, not all of which are found in the guidance documents. Significant environmental harm is important, he notes, as is the public concern aroused by an event such as a major spill. Any perception that the derelictions are motivated by greed, such as trying to operate without upgrading so as to maximize profit, can make a matter criminal. If a civil investigation uncovers false filings or statements, efforts to cover up, or directions to employees to stonewall, then the matter is likely to turn criminal, with those actions becoming additional counts in the indictment. And, says Riesel, "There is always the prosecutor cloaked in hubris or imbued with the belief that he is 'doing the Lord's work on Earth,' who is motivated by a myopic determination to enforce the environmental ethic on corporate America through vigorous use of the criminal process."[5]

EPA press releases do not trumpet the cases that result in acquittals or the prosecutions initially portrayed as crusades against major criminals that are later, quietly, bargained down to a slap on the wrist or tossed out by courts.[6]

The Environmental Law Institute's *ELI Deskbook*, written by lawyers from a prominent defense firm, agrees that "in many instances, there has been little difference between the cases that Justice has prosecuted criminally and those that have proceeded civilly—other than the decisionmaker's intuition as to whether a case warranted indictment."[7]

A federal prosecutor defined the criteria for deciding whether to proceed as "When the little hairs on the back of your neck stand up, it's a felony. When it just makes you tingle, it's a misdemeanor. If it does nothing to you at all, it's a civil problem."[8] Under such standards, prosecutors choose enforcement instruments on the basis of a subjective view of the offender's character as a human being. Anyone who argues too hard is unlikely to be regarded as a good person. Also in jeopardy is anyone who questions the EPA staff's intelligence or good faith, and anyone who contends that economic concerns might be as important as environmental ones.

Some lawyers comment that one of the more difficult aspects of private law practice is maintaining the appropriate level of groveling to government officials, and a criminologist speaking at a legal education seminar noted the difficulty of working with business defendants: "Most of these clients have been upstanding citizens, have been involved in charities and community causes, and generally will have tremendous difficulty identifying with the reality of being charged with a criminal offense. The client may be indignant, even outraged, that he is being investigated, and he will often want to make this known." The speaker went on to say that the lawyer's task is to keep the client from "transmitting a negative initial impression to the court."[9]

The speaker then moved on to advice for dealing with the probation officer who will have a crucial role in recommending sentence. "The client must take responsibility for his actions. He must also provide a sense of how he feels about the offense, e.g., remorse for transgressions, concern for victims if applicable. There should not be any excuses made. All too often, the defendant wants to explain how he is not really guilty, but had no choice except to take the deal offered by the government." This, noted the speaker, only increased the chances of a stiff sentence.[10]

In short, anyone who rubs the agency the wrong way—which usually means anyone who does not seem to share the enforcer's world view or value system—will wind up in deep trouble. This conclusion applies not only to penalties for major pollution but also to violations involving small or nonexistent releases. Even then, anyone who says, "I was making steel or oil or food and I thought that was more important than filling out your form or complying with the last tenth of a percent of your requirement" is on a short cut to jail.

The *ELI Deskbook* emphasizes the politicized nature of the process:

> On close issues, reasonable people will disagree. For every decision not to indict, proponents of prosecution can accurately point to the cases in which similar facts led to criminal charges. In such subjective decisions, it is difficult for the official to provide a concrete explanation that will satisfy all critics. And there is no way to resolve policy disputes by recourse to neutral principles.
>
> In the final analysis, the indeterminate nature of environmental crimes has contributed heavily to the politicization

of the program. In their efforts to avoid giving violators arguments against indictment, prosecutors have rendered themselves defenseless against critics.[11]

A recent report by the General Accounting Office also noted that practices differ substantially among the EPA regions, and that how a company is treated may depend on the unwritten priorities of the particular regional office with which it is dealing.[12]

The Consequences of Arbitrary Enforcement

Abitrary enforcement of environmental regulation not only offends one's sense of justice, it undermines the regulatory enterprise itself.

First, there can be such a thing as *over*enforcement. By subjecting businesses and their officers to heavy penalties even for minor violations, including those that do not cause or even threaten a release of pollutants, the agency does indeed ensure that businesses will devote huge sums to preventing violations. The results are not necessarily positive. As Roger Marzulla, former assistant attorney general in charge of the Environment and Natural Resources Division, puts it,

> It is not surprising that a repressive regime of apparently arbitrary and unjust federal regulatory prosecutions has led businessmen and individual citizens to operate defensively in their dealings with agencies. The compliance officer . . . must sign the myriad reports and applications that must be submitted almost daily to federal agencies. He knows that a single mistake on one such document can land him in federal prison. The result is the focusing of enormous resources on the technical details of compliance with paperwork and similar requirements—often at the expense of huge possible gains in productivity, worker safety and public health which could otherwise be achieved. A frightened, defensive company is not the model of our dynamic system, which has brought this nation the highest standard of living in the world.[13]

Second, because companies have substantial incentives to be safe and defensive, they have little interest in developing new or more efficient methods of controlling pollution. The failure of a new method would leave them open to substantial penalties. As a result,

23

the boom in U.S. investment in new technologies in almost every conceivable area has an important exception—investment in new pollution control technology is almost nonexistent.[14]

Third, arbitrary enforcement tends to encourage lawbreaking because business acceptance of the modern environmental ethic depends in part upon reasonableness. If enforcement seems motivated by whimsy or spite, then legitimacy is lost and people begin to think harder about dodging compliance. EPA efforts to maintain total discretion, based on fear that industries will find tricky ways to evade the intent of a rule, can have the effect of converting a cooperative population into a resentful one that must indeed be ruled by the lash of harsh enforcement rather than by suasion. Roger Marzulla captured the essence of this problem when he wrote,

> When an individual faces the same federal prison time for improperly filling out a required form that a rapist or drug dealer receives, he is justified in questioning the legal system which criminalizes his relatively benign actions. Unjust imprisonment—a staple of repressive governments and police states—may engender fear of the law, but not respect for it. Yet today in the United States the ordinary law-abiding citizen runs the risk of violating one of thousands of complicated (and even conflicting) regulatory requirements, with federal prison as the consequence. This is simply un-American and unacceptable to anyone who believes in the true purpose and genius of the law as an expression of our noblest societal and national goals.[15]

3. EPA's Disregard of Intent

Under some circumstances, the uncertainty and confusion surrounding EPA's rules would not be a serious problem for the regulated community. If the government were required to establish that a defendant knew of the illegality of his action before imposing criminal or civil penalties—or at least could have learned the requirements if he had made reasonable inquiry—the issue would evaporate. In addition, the rules would soon become a good bit plainer quite quickly because EPA's incentives would be for clarity rather than obscurantism.

However, the historic requirement of the criminal law that a defendant is guilty only if he intended his action has been substantially diluted.

It is an axiom of the criminal law that to be guilty of a criminal offense the defendant must have intended to commit the crime. This requirement is softened by the commonsense corollary that he is presumed to understand and intend the usual and natural consequences of his act. He cannot claim that he did not know that pointing a gun at someone and pulling the trigger would cause a lethal projectile to be emitted (*but*, if the defendant were an aborigine who had never seen a gun, then he could indeed defend himself on the ground that he lacked intent to harm). Nor can a defendant evade the penalties by claiming he did not know that shooting people was against the law. For most offenses, this general intent—the intent to perform the physical act—is all that is necessary to complete the offense. The point is often made that the act is *malum in se*, bad in itself, and that the defendant should have known that it was illegal or, even if he did not, that he knew he was doing something wrong and that it does not offend the sense of justice to punish him.

As regulation has increased and the number of regulatory offenses has multiplied, courts have sometimes been reluctant to apply the concept of general intent. The ancient distinction is that many regulatory offenses are *malum prohibitum*, bad only because they are prohibited, and that the normal person may, reasonably, be unaware of the illegality. For these cases, the doctrine of specific intent has been crafted, meaning that the defendant must be aware that his action was indeed illegal before he can be convicted. Tax law is a bastion of specific intent. To be convicted of tax fraud, it must be clear that a taxpayer knows what he was supposed to pay and deliberately did not do so.

The Regulatory Battle over Intent

Regulators dislike the requirement that specific intent exist. They argue that defendants should have known enough to discover whether the conduct was illegal, and that the failure to do so is enough to damn them.

This argument is not totally disreputable; the idea of "inquiry notice"—that someone should have known enough to find out about something—has a long legal pedigree. The courts have responded to it sympathetically. The leading environmental case is the Supreme Court's 1971 decision in *International Minerals*.[1] The Court held that environmental crimes are classified as "public welfare" offenses, which means that a defendant's knowledge that he is dealing with a substance known to be dangerous and thus likely to be regulated is sufficient to support the conviction. The Court noted that mistake of fact might be a defense, though, and that a defendant might be acquitted if, for example, he thought that the substance he was handling was plain water rather than a dangerous chemical.

The "public welfare" doctrine has become a battleground in many contexts, and prosecutors at the DOJ strive to expand its scope. In 1994, the Supreme Court blunted a multipronged DOJ offensive to limit prosecutors' need to prove intent in a series of four cases in which the Court ruled that the government must show specific, not general, intent.[2] These decisions have not been very helpful to environmental defendants, however, because environmental statutes use the standard that violations must be "knowing," not "willful," which courts interpret as meaning that general intent is sufficient.[3] The Fifth Circuit allowed the mistake-of-fact defense hinted at by the Supreme Court in the *International Minerals* case, in *United States v. Ahmad*, in which the defendant contended that he thought he was discharging water rather than gasoline.[4] But in *United States v. Weitzenhoff*, the Ninth Circuit rejected the relevance of the argument that defendants honestly thought that their discharges were allowable under their permit, and the Supreme Court denied review.[5] In legal theory, denials of certiorari by the Supreme Court are not judgments on the merits, so the *Weitzenhoff* defense remains a possibility, outside of the Ninth Circuit. However, the denial followed by only a year the four cases turning back prosecutorial hyperaggression in other areas, so the Court's refusal to take the case can be read as a deliberate decision to leave the environmental prosecutors unchecked. Most courts of appeals have followed this line, applying by rote the *International Minerals* public welfare doctrine.[6]

Part of the problem in the intent cases derives from the old legal maxim that hard cases make bad law, combined with the reality that arguments about intent are often the last desperate gambit of the guilty. In *United States v. Hopkins*,[7] the defendant was caught diluting waste water samples with tap water to avoid permit violations under the Clean Water Act. There was little question of the defendant's knowledge of the law because he had previously signed a consent order. But the trial judge instructed the jury that the defendant's awareness of the law was not a relevant factor, and this became a ground of appeal. The Second Circuit upheld the trial court, which was unfortunate, because it is extraordinarily unlikely that the defendant would have been acquitted under a correct instruction.

Similarly, in *United States v. Kelly*, the Seventh Circuit said, "The jury was required to find that the defendant Kelly knowingly transported a substance that fit within the parameters of the definition of 'hazardous waste,' as defined by Congress, not that Kelly had knowledge that the material was hazardous, and that he had knowledge that the material was waste."[8] This seems an unfortunately broad statement, but reading the facts of the case would lead any reasonable person to conclude that Kelly knew exactly what he was doing and that no jury would credit his claim of ignorance.

Both *Hopkins* and *Kelly* look like cases in which an appellate court got lured into a bad statement of the law because it wanted to avoid a meaningless retrial. Even *Ahmad*, in which the Fifth Circuit allowed the mistake-of-fact defense, does not present a sympathetic case for the defendant. Ahmad put the hose of a motorized pump into an 8,000-gallon tank of gasoline, put the other end into a sewer, started it up, and left for five hours. The pump removed 5,220 gallons of fluid, of which 4,690 gallons were gasoline. Ahmad said he thought he was only siphoning off the water at the bottom of the tank, a tale which, on the evidence, no reasonable jury would have credited for a moment.

Unfortunately, the statements of law in cases such as *Hopkins* and *Kelly* to the effect that proof of intent is not necessary for a criminal conviction are like loaded guns ready for use by the government against defendants with much more plausible claims. The injustices these rules wreak are unlikely to come to light because it is improbable that a future defendant will go to trial knowing that the case law is stacked against him.[9]

EPA's Disregard of Intent: The *Hanousek* Case

To put the controversy over intent in human terms and to show how troublesome the system has become, consider a recent case that has aroused the business community: *United States v. Hanousek*, in which the Ninth Circuit affirmed a conviction of a supervisor at Pacific and Arctic Pipelines, Inc. (P&A) for criminal violations of the Clean Water Act.[10] The trial court gave the defendant six months in jail, six months in a halfway house, and six months of supervised release. The sentence was bumped up on the basis of Hanousek's "role as a supervisor in a criminal activity."

EPA described the case in its 1997 "Enforcement Accomplishments Report" as one in which "Hanousek was supervising the illegal removal of rock from U.S. Forest Service land" when a piece of equipment struck an oil pipeline and caused the release of between 1,000 and 5,000 gallons of oil into the Skagway River.[11] Some additional facts about the case can be found in EPA's 1996 "Enforcement Accomplishments Report,"[12] which states that two P&A companies were sentenced to pay $1.5 million in fines and restitution costs and were placed on five years of probation as a result of the incident. They also agreed to clean up several contaminated sites along a historic rail route. One of the P&A companies was also convicted of stealing rock from U.S. Forest Service land and of transporting hazardous waste into Canada, but it is not clear what connection this had to the oil spill.

The story, as provided in the trial and appellate opinions, plus EPA's documents, can be pieced together as follows.

Hanousek was a roadmaster employed by the P&A Railway, and thus "was responsible for every detail of safe and efficient maintenance and construction" on his stretch of road. An above-ground oil pipeline ran next to the track. The project that caused the trouble involved blasting rock outcroppings next to the railroad and putting the fractured rock onto rail cars with a backhoe. The project was contracted out and, to protect the pipeline, the contractor covered a 300-foot section of the line with railroad ties and sand. The work site was 1,000 feet long, and after Hanousek took over supervision, no further pipeline was covered. However, a work platform of sand and gravel was placed over the pipeline for the backhoe to use.

One evening, when Hanousek was not at the site, the backhoe operator noticed that some loose rocks had been caught by the plow of a departed train and dragged to a location just off the tracks near the unprotected pipeline. The operator drove his backhoe off of the working platform down the tracks about 50 or 100 yards and tried to sweep the rocks away from the tracks with the backhoe bucket. He hit the pipeline, causing a rupture.

Hanousek was convicted of a criminal violation of the Clean Water Act for negligently discharging a harmful quantity of oil. He was acquitted of a charge of conspiring to provide false information to the Coast Guard. A P&A officer, Paul Taylor, was also charged with negligent discharge, and several counts of making false statements and obstruction of justice. He was convicted, however, on only two counts of·making false statements. Apparently, he did not appeal. As a result, the case reports contain no information on the crimes the two were alleged to have committed during the investigation.[13]

Under the Clean Water Act, negligent discharge of a substance is a criminal offense. The issues on appeal were threefold. First, is "simple negligence" sufficient to support a conviction versus the "gross deviation from the standard of care" usually required for criminal negligence? On this point, the Ninth Circuit held that Congress intended simple negligence to be enough. Second, did a simple negligence standard offend due process? The answer was "no"; anyone who deals with public hazards can be held to this standard. Further, the CWA is a public welfare law, and the defendant need not have knowledge of the law or intend to violate it. Intent requirements are satisfied if the defendant knows he is dealing with a noxious material. Third, could Hanousek be held vicariously liable

OUT OF BOUNDS AND OUT OF CONTROL

for the action of the backhoe operator? The court found that he could be convicted only for his own negligence. But it regarded the following evidence as sufficient to support a jury verdict that Hanousek was negligent:

> After Hanousek took over responsibility for the project . . . no further sections of the pipeline along the work site were protected. . . . Finally, the government presented evidence that although the rock quarrying work had been completed in the location of the rupture, rocks would sometimes fall off loaded railroad cars as they proceeded through completed sections of the work site; that no policy prohibited the use of backhoes off the work platform.

This is an appalling case.

First, the oil spill was not a significant incident; 5,000 gallons (the high end of the court's range) is a little more than half the size of a retail service station tank. EPA takes the view that *any* petroleum spill is serious. EPA says, "One pint of oil released into the water can spread and cover one acre of water surface area and seriously damage an aquatic habitat."[14] This may be true technically, but oil degrades rapidly and does little lasting harm. This is a good thing, because in 1997, 8,624 reported incidents of oil spills into U.S. waters resulted in the release of 942 million gallons of oil, and 54 of them involved releases of between 1,000 and 5,000 gallons of oil.[15] Waterways and ocean beds are also subject to numerous natural releases, but no numerical estimates are available. Obviously, the oil spill into the Skagway River was regrettable, but hardly catastrophic. And P&A had already paid heavily for the cleanup and damages. On balance, the government reaction seems out of all proportion to fault or harm, especially because running a railroad and piping heating oil to Alaska are worthy enterprises and the people involved in them are fulfilling an important social function and contributing to the betterment of humanity.

Second, it is impossible to understand wherein Hanousek was negligent. The appellate court seemed to assume that he had taken no steps to prevent the use of the backhoe away from the area where the pipeline was not covered. But the existence of a policy against using the backhoe in uncovered areas is readily implied by the fact that the pipeline *was* covered where the backhoe was working. One cannot help but imagine that the government told the backhoe operator, "You will be at the trial—as a defendant, or as a witness against your superiors—take your pick," which could certainly have affected his memory on whether he had violated standing instructions. The appellate court also assumed that Hanousek was negligent for not ordering the pipeline covered over the entire 1,000-foot project area. But this is a dubious proposition. Covering and then uncovering the pipeline would require work with heavy machinery in constant proximity to the 1,000-foot-long work site. The risk of accidental rupture might well be higher from this activity than from covering the pipeline only in the immediate vicinity of the backhoe work. The appellate court shrugged off this issue on the ground that it had, presumably, been argued in front of the jury. But who would want to have his freedom depend on the ability of 12 lay jurors to decide on complex technical issues of pipeline safety practices?

There is a real doubt that *anyone* was negligent, even the backhoe operator when he tried to move the rocks. Rocks near a rail line create a situation that is dangerous to both trains and a pipeline. In June 2000, EPA fined the Union Pacific Railroad $800,000 for seven derailments that caused the discharge of chemicals, including diesel fuel from locomotive fuel tanks, into navigable waters. Two of the derailments were due to rocks on the track, and as part of the settlement the railroad agreed to a comprehensive project to mitigate the hazards of falling rock.[16] In the *Hanousek* case, the operator might well have decided that the rocks presented a menace and needed to be moved immediately. Because his execution was poor does not mean that his decision was wrong.

A third problem involves the government's choice of charges. The government indicted Hanousek on one count of negligent discharge and one count of making false statements. Hanousek's superior, Taylor, was charged with one count of negligent discharge, one count of failing to report a discharge, one count of conspiracy to make false statements, five counts of making false statements, and one count of obstructing justice. From this welter of accusations, Hanousek was convicted only of negligent discharge, and Taylor was convicted on two of the false statement counts. In addition, consider the strange references in the EPA material to the crime of stealing rocks from the Forest Service. It sounds as if the government charged them with criminal conduct for cleaning up rock debris, a charge that can have no purpose—aside from pure malice—except to raise the risks to the defendant and to raise the price of a plea bargain or financial settlement.

Finally, consider the sentencing. Federal guidelines say that the trial judge may add to the sentence if the defendant supervised one or more participants. The *Hanousek* trial judge noted that a participant is someone who is "criminally responsible for the commission of the offense," even if he was not prosecuted. The Ninth Circuit said that the backhoe operator was a participant even though he was not prosecuted, and Hanousek supervised the whole project. Ergo, the augmentation was proper.

This part of the opinion is particularly disturbing. According to the appellate court, Hanousek could be convicted only for *his own* negligence. There was no basis for concluding that the backhoe operator was negligent because this issue was not tried. But if the backhoe operator was not negligent, then how could he have been a "participant," as was required for the augmentation of Hanousek's sentence? This case is almost certainly not the type envisioned by the drafters of the sentencing guidelines, and to pile the augmentation for supervision on top of negligence was clearly unjust.

It is impossible to avoid the conclusion that something was going on in the *Hanousek* case that is not set forth in the case reports. The most likely possibility is that the government decided Hanousek had given them false statements, so they severely punished him. But these charges did not result in a conviction, so obviously the jury did not think the defendant guilty of them.

One is left with the overall impression of a vindictive government, irritated at its inability to prove charges of false statements or obstruction of justice, and satisfied to rely on the distortions and confusions of the public welfare doctrine to put someone in jail for conduct that does not appear particularly blameworthy. That the government's action was approved by the Ninth Circuit and its appeal rejected by the Supreme Court makes the whole episode even more unsavory.[17]

David Stirling of the Pacific Legal Foundation points out the contradiction between the government's harsh treatment of Hanousek and its infinitely forgiving attitude toward its own employees. In May 2000, shortly after the Supreme Court refused to hear Hanousek's appeal, an employee of the U.S. Forest Service ignored unfavorable weather forecasts and lit what was intended to be a controlled burn in the Los Alamos National Forest. The fire blew out of control, burning 47,000 acres of forestland and causing hundreds of millions of dollars of damage. Interior Secretary Bruce Babbitt said that no criminal action would be taken because "You do not prosecute people for making mistakes." As Stirling notes, this may be how the government treats its own, but Edward Hanousek is in jail even though he was at home in bed when an employee of a subcontractor made a mistake. Further, the spill involved in the Hanousek case did trivial damage compared with the disaster in Los Alamos.[18]

Harsh law for the governed and infinite leniency for the governors puts a new twist on the meaning of "the rule of law."

4. The Inscrutability of Regulatory Requirements

Because of their lack of success in contesting intent, defendants have developed a related argument that may better fit the realities of the regulatory state. It is based on the Due Process Clause of the U.S. Constitution and section 552 of the Administrative Procedures Act, and takes the form of a contention that the defendant lacked fair notice of the law.[1] That is, even if a defendant knew that he was operating in a regulated area or dealing with hazardous substances and made an honest effort to ascertain the requirements, he could not reasonably be expected to figure them out.

A major advantage of the "fair notice" argument over the "no intent" argument is that a fair notice requirement would also apply to civil penalties, not just to criminal prosecutions. Intent has always been regarded as irrelevant to civil penalties, which are imposed to encourage people to be careful and to force them to ascertain the relevant rules regardless of criminal intent, so even a revised and improved standard requiring that intent be proven before criminal conviction would not save respondents from ruinous civil penalties for violating laws of which they have no knowledge.

But a fair notice principle would provide a shield against unjust civil penalties because, as one court put it in 1980, when penalties are at stake under any rubric, "fundamental fairness requires that the regulation be so clear that men of common intelligence need not guess at the meaning and differ as to the application."[2]

Fair Notice and the Courts

The concept that fair notice is required finds support from the Supreme Court in *United States v. Pennsylvania Chemical Co.*[3] In that case, the Court held that a defendant charged with a criminal violation of an act must be allowed to present evidence that he had been misled by regulators about the meaning of the law. The government argued that the defendant should have known that the regulatory information he received from the agency was mistaken.

The D.C. Circuit is the leader in developing a fair notice doctrine. In the most important case, *General Electric Co. v. EPA*,[4] GE was charged with violating polychlorinated biphenyl (PCB) regulations because it distilled chemicals before disposing of them. The pertinent regulations, said the court, "not only . . . failed clearly to bar distillation, they apparently permitted it," and the agency had set a "regulatory trap." It could not punish GE for falling into it.

The most recent D.C. Circuit affirmation of the fair notice principle is in *United States v. Chrysler*,[5] which involved a recall of automobiles by the National Highway Traffic Safety Administration. The court wrote:

> In *General Electric Co. v. EPA*, 53 F.3d 1324, 1328, 1333 (D.C. Cir. 1995), we held that, because "[d]ue process requires that parties receive fair notice before being deprived of property," the Environmental Protection Agency (EPA) could not penalize General Electric for asserted regulatory violations when General Electric lacked "fair warning of [EPA's] interpretation of the regulations." We made it clear that, "[i]n the absence of notice—for example, where the regulation is not sufficiently clear to warn a party about what is expected of it—an agency may not deprive a party of property," particularly when "the interpretation is so far from a reasonable person's understanding of the regulations that they could not have fairly informed [the regulated party] of the agency's perspective." *Id.* at 1328, 1330; *see also Rollins Envtl. Servs. Inc. v. EPA*, 937 F.2d 649, 652 n.2 (D.C. Cir. 1991) ("[A] regulation carrying penal sanctions must give fair warning of the conduct it prohibits or requires.") (citation omitted); *id.* at 654 n.1 (Edwards, J., dissenting in part and concurring in part) ("It is basic hornbook law in the administrative context that 'the application of a regulation in a particular situation may be challenged on the ground that it does not give fair warning that the allegedly violative conduct was prohibited.' ") (citation omitted); *Satellite Broad. Co. v. FCC*, 824 F.2d 1, 3 (D.C. Cir. 1987) ("Traditional concepts of due process incorporated into administrative law preclude an agency from penalizing a private party for violating a rule without first providing adequate notice of the substance of the rule."); *Gates and Fox Co. v. OSHRC*, 790 F.2d 154, 156 (D.C. Cir. 1986) ("[T]he due process clause prevents . . . the application of a regulation that fails to give fair warning of the conduct it prohibits or requires.").

The Fourth Circuit upheld a fair notice defense in 1997, in *U.S. v. Hoechst-Celanese Corporation (HCC)*.[6] A large factor in the decision was that HCC consulted a state agency concerning the meaning of the relevant rule and was informed that the company was exempt. The state agency was interpreting a letter written by EPA Region VI, which was aware of the state view and did not contradict it. Subsequently, a different EPA region (Region IV) interpreted the rule more restrictively than did Region VI and the state, and brought an enforcement action against the company for similar emissions from a plant in Region IV.

However, the court in *HCC* ruled that the fair notice defense terminated when EPA informed the company that it was adopting Region IV's interpretation of the applicable rule, even though that interpretation was far from self-evident. Consequently, although the case affords protection against the worst abuses, it provides no shield for the time it takes a defendant to get a definitive resolution concerning the meaning of the law, even if there is a dispute within EPA.

If a major interpretation is issued through normal rulemaking, an affected industry can appeal it before it becomes effective, and have the issues clarified without opening itself up to penalties. In *HCC*, the dissent points out that there were strong indications that the agency was in fact adopting an interpretation at odds with its own intention at the time of the rule's promulgation, and it was fundamentally unfair to subject the company to penalties while it sought to get the issue resolved definitively: "While I agree with the majority that Hoechst Celanese had notice of the position of EPA Region IV in August 1989, this notice should not, against the background of inconsistent EPA interpretations over time and throughout the different regions, constitute a definitive agency-wide EPA notice that such penalties could be imposed for non-compliance with one interpretation."[7]

In such a system, it becomes exceedingly difficult for a citizen to resist even an extremely dubious agency interpretation of a rule. If the meter on civil penalties and possible criminal prosecution starts running as soon as a company is informed of the EPA's position, then the risks associated with challenging the agency's interpretation become overwhelming. Enforcement officials are adept at exploiting the fear of these risks to expand their authority, and at retaliating against people who question it.[8]

The Case for Regulatory Fair Warning

Outside of the D.C. Circuit, few courts of appeal have addressed the fair notice issue, but Congress is beginning to stir. In the 106th Congress, House member George W. Gekas (R-Pa.) and 25 cosponsors introduced H.R. 881, the Regulatory Fair Warning Act (RFWA), which would require that sanctions not be imposed for violation of an agency rule if the rule was not "knowable to a person who has engaged in a reasonable good faith investigation of the rules applicable to the conduct that allegedly violated the rule," if the rule "failed to give fair warning of the conduct the rule prohibits or requires," or if the person relied on written representations by an agency or official. This last protection is intended to deal with the (increasingly common) situation in which a person seeks and receives advice from an agency official only to be prosecuted when other parts of the agency decide that the advice was incorrect.

The Clinton administration opposed the RFWA, alternatively denying that there was a problem or asserting that it had been fixed. In 1995, the Chairman of the Subcommittee on the Constitution of the House Committee on the Judiciary posed a number of queries to the DOJ, attempting to solicit *some* expression of concern for issues of intent and fair notice. He asked whether a regulated company should be pursued for penalties if it had in good faith tried to comply, if it had relied on an erroneous interpretation supplied by an agency, or if the interpretation of a rule had changed. In each case, DOJ's answer remained that such factors could be considered by the agency, at its discretion, in deciding whether to bring a case and in assessing the amount of the penalty, but they should not be available as defenses to defeat the action.[9] In response to other queries, DOJ defended the EPA's total discretion to use unpublished interpretations of laws or rules. It denied the existence of any need to clarify or change any standard governing intent in environmental cases.

In 1998, a Deputy Associate Attorney General represented DOJ at hearings on the proposed Regulatory Fair Warning Act (H.R. 4049, at the time). He opposed it adamantly, saying that there are "better ways" to ensure fair notice, such as the action by Congress to "expressly provide by statute that good faith compliance efforts should be considered . . . by courts and agencies in determining the assessment of any civil penalty," and agency efforts at education.[10]

At further hearings in 1999, Chairman Gekas characterized the DOJ position:

> I will also invite the Justice Department to express its views once again, with the hope that it will agree to support and work for fair warning legislation. The Department has been half-hearted in its support of fairness so far. And its unwillingness to come forward with concrete proposals to ensure regulatory fairness, leaves me—and, I think, the American people—deeply unsatisfied. I hope and believe that this will change.[11]

Why Chairman Gekas believes DOJ's attitude will change is a mystery. It would be hard to find clearer statements that enforcers believe they should have untrammeled authority to exercise power according to whim than the Deputy Associate Attorney General's statements. The regulatory officials are not merely indifferent to the rule of law; they actively oppose it.

5. Retroactive Rulemaking through Enforcement

Courts have often said that agencies can interpret their laws and regulations during enforcement litigation, sometimes noting that such action seems anomalous and leads to "adjudicatory ad hocery." But they then add that the power is nonetheless enshrined in the law.[1]

This practice of rulemaking through enforcement is a particularly pernicious kind of retroactive lawmaking. In legal theory, the agency is not *making* law when it interprets a statute or rule in the course of an enforcement proceeding; it is merely *explaining* what the rule always meant, even if this meaning was not visible to the naked eye. In practice, EPA has adopted a policy of using the enforcement process to revise and extend laws and regulations, a development with serious implications for the tattered concept of the rule of law. The agency decides that some conduct *should* have violated the law, even if no extant rule covers it, so it reinterprets an old rule as applying to the past conduct. Or EPA learns that companies are interpreting an ambiguous rule in a manner of which the agency disapproves. So the agency issues an interpretation and applies it retrospectively, not just prospectively, arguing that it has only "clarified" what was always the companies' duty.

The action is usually accompanied by a press release excoriating the targeted industry for its environmental recalcitrance, as if the law had been clear all along and the industry's actions deliberately nefarious. A rationale underlying EPA's cases also seems to be that every company should be bound to emulate EPA's single-value emphasis on an environmental ethic. No one has a right to pay attention to any other value, such as cost or efficiency, in interpreting EPA rules.

EPA finds this ad hoc rulemaking through the enforcement process an efficient means of expanding its regulatory reach. It also relieves the agency of any need to follow the procedures established by the Administrative Procedures Act and specific substantive statutes, such as the requirements that notices be published in the *Federal Register*, that interested parties be allowed to comment, that the agency prepare a statement of basis and purpose explaining the reasoning behind the rule, and that this statement respond to any cogent comments received. Formal action also requires preparation of bothersome impact statements, including analyses of economic issues and of the impact on small business.

Rulemaking through enforcement short-circuits those annoying (to the agency) requirements to justify its decisions. It also deprives the regulated community of an opportunity to participate in the decision, and deprives the agency of the benefit of comments from the regulated community, comments that can actually help regulators who lack experience in running facilities or in complying with regulations.

The New Source Review Controversy

With great fanfare, the Department of Justice, acting on behalf of EPA, filed suit against seven electric utilities on November 3, 1999. At the same time, EPA issued an administrative complaint against the Tennessee Valley Authority, a federal government agency.[2]

The accompanying press release charged that "17 of the companies' power plants illegally released massive amounts of air pollutants for years, which have contributed to some of the most severe environmental problems in the United States today" because they had made major modifications without installing required pollution control equipment. They had, "for years," said the release, "operated without the best available emissions control technology," in contravention of the law. Under the statute, civil penalties for this offense can be as high as $25,000 per day before January 30, 1997, and $27,500 per day thereafter, and the government promised to seek "significant" penalties from all of the offenders. A little arithmetic indicates that the defendants could be facing penalties of $9,125,000 per plant per year for many years, so the stakes are considerable.

Subsequently, the cases were expanded to cover even more of the defendants' plants. Once again, respondents were charged with "illegally releasing massive amounts of air pollutants for years, contributing to some of the most severe environmental problems facing the nation today."[3] EPA also promised to seek heavy civil penalties and, during the expansion, it announced a settlement with one of the smaller targets. Tampa Electric agreed to adopt a package of emissions reductions, forfeit valuable emissions credits, pay $3.5 million in penalties, and spend up to $11 million on "environmentally beneficial projects."[4] In late 2000, Cinergy Corp. agreed to an $8 million fine, $21.5 million in environmental projects, and more than $1 billion worth of environmental improvements.[5]

The utilities are only the first on a list of targets. EPA also has its sights on the nation's petroleum refiners, the pulp and paper industry, and possibly others.[6]

EPA press releases make the New Source Review (NSR) dispute sound like a conspiracy by a group of scofflaws. But the full story is more complicated. Describing the NSR dispute requires a reminder of some fundamental truths about the origins of the nation's environmental laws.

For complex political and sociological reasons, moral vehemence was dominant during the surge of legislative energy that produced the environmental laws, and for about 15 years Congress passed one anti-pollution law after another. Each time, it avoided providing explicit directions on how EPA was to make the unavoidable tradeoffs between environmental values and other values.

The Clean Air Act provides a good example. From a health perspective it would seem that less of a pollutant is obviously better. This is a naive view because, in fact, improvement in health depends on what we must give up to get to "less." A freezing man sitting in front of a fire can reduce his health risks from smoke inhalation by putting out the fire. However, this act will improve his health only in the sense that his frozen carcass will not suffer any lung damage. The world is a complex set of tradeoffs, and single-minded focus on any one factor is a road to disaster.

The principles governing the homely smoke-and-fire case also govern pollution control on a macro scale. During the preindustrial Stone Age, human life expectancy was about 18 years. Any effort to produce perfect health by eliminating all pollution would, in fact, be destructive.

No one in Congress ever really thought that the nation's health or welfare would be improved, for example, by shutting down its electrical generating capacity or even a significant piece of it. Some years ago, during an argument in front of the D.C. Circuit, environmental plaintiffs were arguing for a very strict interpretation of the

Clean Air Act. A government lawyer responded by noting that the plaintiffs' position would require most of American industry to shut down, a fact mentioned nowhere in the legislative debates leading up to the law. "If Congress really intended this," the lawyer said dryly, "I think someone would have said something about it at the time."[7]

So Congress does not mandate that standards for air quality be set at zero pollution, but at a level that protects the "public health with an adequate margin of safety." This leaves serious questions, such as, When is the public health protected? At zero level? When no catastrophe occurs? Somewhere in between? And what is "adequate" or "margin of safety"? Congress answered none of these questions explicitly. Even at its most political, though, Congress recognized that environmental concerns could not be allowed to automatically supersede economic concerns. The legislative history of the Clean Air Act, for example, shows clearly that "Congress sought to accommodate the conflict between the economic interest in permitting capital improvements to continue and the environmental interest in improving air quality."[8]

Unfortunately, Congress was incapable of making a straightforward statement that tough choices must be made and this fact is simply part of the human condition. Congress adopted various subterfuges to accomplish its objective of maintaining economic sanity without diluting the appearance of its total commitment to the environment. Sometimes it carved out specific exemptions from statutes, such as the exclusions of petroleum products from coverage by Superfund.[9] In other instances, Congress inserted limitations phrased in terms of risk or on the basis of the practicality or availability of technology.[10]

In the Clean Air Act provisions dealing with pollution caused by industrial sources, Congress used the device of technology requirements to limit the demands of environmental protection on the nation's industrial infrastructure. Congress specified that pollution control technology had to be either the Lowest Achievable Emissions Rate (LAER) or the Best Available Control Technology (BACT), depending on the air quality status of the geographic area in which a facility is located.[11]

A second check imposed by Congress on the Clean Air Act's demands on the economy was to differentiate between old and new sources. LAER and BACT were imposed on new sources. Regulation of existing sources was left to different sections of the Clean Air Act, those dealing with the emission of substances classified as "hazardous air pollutants," with the attainment of air quality standards by states, and with the prevention of significant deterioration of air quality in areas that now meet air quality standards.[12] Existing sources are by no means unregulated; they are just not subject to the specific requirements imposed on new sources.

Obviously, such a dichotomy between old and new sources is a compromise designed to reflect competing economic, philosophical, and political interests:

- The economic rationale for treating old sources differently from new sources is that retrofitting control equipment is often more expensive than designing controls from the outset of planning a new facility. If costs are a consideration, as they explicitly are under the NSR program, then it must be recognized that cost factors are fundamentally different for new and old sources.
- The philosophical rationale for treating old sources differently from new sources is to ensure that investors are confident that they will not be treated poorly once a facility is built, that they will not be held to ransom by their sunk costs. If they do not have this confidence they will not build, to the nation's loss.
- The political rationale for treating old sources differently from new sources can be found in the need to solicit industry support for regulation. Established firms are likely to fight laws that impose stiff economic costs on their operations but are less likely to fight (and indeed are likely to support) laws that impose stiff economic costs on future competitors.

Like any compromise, this one is imperfect, and creates tricky cross-currents of incentives. Favored treatment of old plants encourages owners to keep them operating beyond what would otherwise be their useful life because new plants would be subject to more stringent environmental controls. As an analogy, look at the effect of the strong historical preservation laws that exist in the District of Columbia. Developers tear down an entire building, leaving the facade standing supported by steel scaffolding, while they construct a new building behind it. Operators of industrial plants have an incentive to do the equivalent, contending that as long as the old

45

facade remains, it is an old plant and not a new one. David Hawkins of the Natural Resources Defense Council says that some industry actions labeled as routine maintenance "may remind you of the fabled 'one-hundred-year-old' axe: it's only had two new heads and four new handles over its life."[13]

On the other hand, it is in no one's interest that proper industrial maintenance be discouraged, which means that differentiating between old and new facilities will be immensely difficult. Industrial plants are subject to endless tinkering in the form of routine maintenance, minor modifications, and major upgrades. In the course of a year, for instance, a pulp and paper mill may make 40,000 changes in equipment, procedures, and operations.[14] When do these actions become so major that they trigger the technological requirements of NSR? If any of those changes are deemed to transform an old source into a new source, then it will take at least 18 months for the permit to be reviewed and granted, a delay which could well mean that the plant would be required to shut down. It is not surprising that only 250 sources apply for an NSR permit each year, out of 20,000 that are classified by EPA as "major."[15]

Drawing the lines necessary to carry out the congressional mandate on NSR requirements would tax the abilities of the most impartial of agencies, especially given the vague language of the statute. The most recent version of the law was passed in 1977, and in 1980 EPA promulgated a 20-page regulation. In years since, EPA has provided more than 4,000 pages of guidance trying to explain the rule.[16] For the past decade, the EPA Office of Air and Radiation has been conducting a dialogue with the regulated industries on how to implement the NSR requirements. EPA officials openly disagree not only over what the requirements should be but also over what they are.[17]

At the beginning of this process, EPA seemed interested in reconciling the environmental and economic goals implicit in the NSR standards.[18] A Tennessee Valley Authority (TVA) official commented on the situation before the EPA filed suit:

> Although there has been some criticism of its complexity, TVA believes the NSR program has generally been a success. EPA has largely applied the program's requirements in a way that does not impede routine maintenance of the nation's electric utility generating resources. Moreover, in the past the program has not been applied in a way to discourage improvements in unit efficiency and reliability.[19]

In recent years, however, EPA's Enforcement Division (as opposed to the Office of Air and Radiation) has assumed responsibility for the matter and has adopted a broad interpretation of what constitutes a "new source" for regulatory purposes, an interpretation that incorporates even practices that might fairly be deemed routine maintenance. The new interpretation put an end to 25 years of wary cooperation between the regulated and regulating communities and imposed this new definition of what constitutes a new source retroactively.[20] EPA can leverage this new interpretation both to pressure the industry to desist from court challenges to the rule (if they lose, they pay for every day the challenge dragged on) and to extract a great deal of money from the companies as the price of not being shut down.

Furthermore, turning the interpretation of the laws over to the enforcers has a significant public relations advantage. As noted, the press release accompanying the suit against the electric utilities portrays the industries as total scofflaws. The public reader does not get any sense that this is a dispute over the meaning of a law, that there are interests on each side, and that, in the companies' views, EPA is attempting to use the threat of civil penalties to bludgeon them into accepting an interpretation of the law that does not reflect the understanding at the time of passage. As two experts recently wrote,

> While EPA's Office of Air and Radiation has struggled since 1992 to revise the complicated NSR structure through a formal rulemaking process, the Office of Enforcement and Compliance Assurance (OECA) has reformed the rules in a matter of months, without regard to public notice and comment requirements.[21]

They also note that the agency fully intends to make its new interpretations retroactive:

> Through its enforcement initiatives to date, EPA has demonstrated that it will seek to apply its interpretation of the routine maintenance exclusion retroactively. The agency is acting as though its position was on the books from the day the routine maintenance exclusion was promulgated. Furthermore, EPA is attempting to ferret out any evidence of modifications through aggressive use of its information

collection powers under the Clean Air Act. In its utility campaign, for instance, the agency demanded sales data from boiler manufacturers from as far back as 1930.[22]

EPA also counts on industry's sense of responsibility and fear of adverse public relations to create pressure to settle these cases. TVA filed in court for a stay of EPA's order in May 2000, noting that it could not now conduct previously scheduled maintenance without running the risk of substantial legal penalties under EPA's new interpretation. Yet, "Postponement of a significant number of these [scheduled] projects could result in severe disruption of the electric service during periods of peak demand in the TVA Region as well as the entire Eastern United States, including those utilities interconnected with the TVA system such as Alabama Power, Georgia Power, and Duke Power."[23]

So if power is in short supply, EPA might well be responsible. But given the agency's superior ability to control the megaphone of the national media, the agency will certainly try, and might succeed, in deflecting public blame for such brownouts. In June 2000, gasoline prices were much higher in the Midwest than in other parts of the nation due to EPA rules requiring the addition of ethanol and special infrastructure problems in the area. EPA demanded an explanation of the higher prices from oil company executives, saying they had offered "no good explanations" and inferring collusion and price gouging.[24]

As this analysis was being prepared, concern over the NSR litigation intensified. The report of the National Energy Policy Development Group (NEPDG) recommended that "The Administrator of the Environmental Protection Agency, in consultation with the Secretary of Energy and other relevant agencies, review New Source Review regulations, including administrative interpretation and implementation, and report to the President within 90 days on the impact of the regulations on investment in new utility and refinery generation capacity, energy efficiency, and environmental protection."[25] EPA's response was due on August 17, 2001.

In the meantime EPA continues to press individual cases, particularly against the petroleum industry.[26]

EPA vs. the Motor Vehicle Industry

EPA has also launched a series of high-profile actions against the automobile industry, repeatedly charging companies with deliberate violations of the Clean Air Act. Each EPA action was accompanied by large-scale publicity about the importance of the case, the nefarious conduct of the company, and the size of the settlement received or the penalty sought. The basic spin was that companies instituted ways to cheat, were caught, and now must pay the price of their perfidy. In reality, for the situations I examined closely, the charges were for actions that were not explicitly prohibited under regulations at the time and that had little or no impact on environmental quality.[27]

Mazda

In 1999, Mazda paid a $900,000 penalty to settle claims that it failed to file an emissions defect report with the agency in timely fashion. It was not clear whether any automobile parts had actually failed, or whether they only had the potential to fail.[28]

Toyota

In July 1999, EPA, acting through the DOJ, sued Toyota for installing pollution control "defeat" devices. It sought $58 billion in civil penalties—$27,500 for each automobile that allegedly violated the law.[29] Lois J. Shiffer, the assistant attorney general for the environment and natural resources at DOJ, said, "Companies that take short cuts with their vehicle pollution control systems shortchange the consumer and our environment. We will hold them accountable."[30] The California Air Resources Board had already acted. In September 1998 it ordered a recall, and when Toyota declined, started formal administrative action. The state accompanied its action with the usual insults, saying that although Toyota's equipment worked properly in the laboratory, it "failed to detect vapor leaks . . . under normal on-road use," and adding that "it is unfortunate that Toyota, which positions itself as an environmentally sensitive company, would resist recalling these vehicles and correcting this problem."[31]

Here is the real story.

EPA requires an automaker to furnish a certificate of conformity describing the vehicle and its emission control system. As part of this control system, the vehicle must be equipped with an on-board diagnostic (OBD) system capable of detecting various malfunctions in the emissions control system, including that part of the system that controls evaporative emissions escaping from the fuel system. The monitor checks hydrocarbon pressure in the Evap system, which should trigger a malfunction indicator light (MIL)—also called the "idiot light"—if a loss of pressure occurs equal to that which would be caused by a 0.04-inch hole anywhere in the system.

California has parallel rules. EPA's rules also provide that compliance can be demonstrated by showing compliance with California regulations governing OBDs (called "OBD II requirements" by EPA). OBD II stipulates that vehicles must have an MIL that alerts the owner of an emissions-related malfunction.

Emissions testing is a formalized process. Cars are tested according to protocols dictated by the EPA or by the state agency. These protocols are, presumably, designed by the agency to serve as proxies for real-world conditions. Toyota's vehicles passed both California- and EPA-mandated tests for emissions. However, California then tried an additional experiment. The state agency found a few (approximately 10) employees of the California EPA who owned Toyotas. The agency punched a 0.04-inch hole in the Evap systems in each of the vehicles, and drove them. The MIL was not triggered, whereupon California EPA sued Toyota for not complying with emission standards.[32]

Toyota is defending itself against the California action on the ground that the state agency's casual empiricism is not the test the company is required to meet and that these results cannot be substituted for the legally required tests that were passed by the company. California cannot simply make up new tests and apply them retroactively. If the state finds that its test protocols do not accurately measure real-world conditions, then it should go back to the drawing board and design new protocols, not sue a company for not passing its newly minted test.[33]

The federal government's complaint alleges that Toyota sold cars that were not covered by the certificates of conformity in two respects:

- When an auto company certifies that its vehicles meet emissions standards, it must describe the conditions that must be met for the OBD system to function. Toyota's certification contained such descriptions, such as stipulations about coolant temperatures and drive times. However, according to the complaint, the Toyota system was subject to additional conditions that were *not* disclosed in its application, involving numbers of stops, fuel consumption, and related factors. These additional conditions "reduce the frequency with which each affected vehicle monitors for Evap system malfunctions." (Note that the complaint does *not* claim that the system fails to detect emissions.)

- Toyota installed a software program, also not described in the certificate of conformity, designed to override the MIL during the first 20 minutes of operation under certain conditions, and which reduced the ability of the vehicle to detect an Evap system malfunction.[34] (Note that an "Evap system malfunction" is not the same as "emissions," nor is it the same as a "flaw," "defect," or even "failure.")

The conclusion is that some of EPA's contentions may be true, technically, if read closely. Toyota isn't saying. Its Web site contains nothing on the federal suit—no press releases, no mention of the case.

Holman Jenkins of the *Wall Street Journal* explains the case as follows.[35] The Evap monitoring system produces too many false positive signals. A loose gasoline cap, an incomplete fuel burn caused by a laboring engine, a momentary loss of traction, or a failure of some other sensor triggers the MIL, telling owners that a problem exists and that the vehicle needs service even when this is not the case. Auto owners have learned this, and have come to treat the idiot light as an extraneous bit of nonsense. Toyota tried to program the system to avoid the false positives so that the MIL was triggered only when a real release of emissions occurs.

If the EPA complaint is read with this possibility in mind, its roundabout phrasing begins to make sense. The complaint never states that the system fails to react to real leaks. It states that the undisclosed conditions "reduce the frequency with which each Affected Vehicle monitors for Evap system malfunctions," and it alleges that Toyota "did not disclose . . . the existence of the software-based device." But the complaint does not allege that real emissions go undetected.

Even the strongest sentence in the complaint should be very carefully parsed. It says that because of Toyota's actions, the "OBD systems rarely monitor for Evap system malfunctions . . . and . . . will rarely illuminate the MIL even when an Evap system malfunction is present." This statement is not the same as charging that the OBD system fails to identify a problem that results in the escape of emissions—"system malfunction" is a broad term, not synonymous with "emissions release." Furthermore, and crucially, if the Evap system has a flaw that is producing a continuing leak, then the monitor does not need to detect each individual "malfunction." An occasional trigger will be enough to alert the driver, *if and only if the system is reliable in that it does not produce false positives.*

From the viewpoint of quality control, ensuring that the MIL is *not* illuminated by false positives is as important as ensuring that it *is* triggered by real problems. Leaving aside any question of whether Toyota technically violated EPA's regulations, the agency should be thanking Toyota for trying to make the system work, not suing it for $58 billion. At most, the situation should prompt consultation between the industry and the EPA with a view toward solving a problem, not imposing a penalty.

EPA vs. the Diesel Engine Industry

The seven largest diesel engine makers were charged with selling engines "equipped with devices designed to defeat federal anti-pollution controls. These defeat devices are really 'deceit' devices. . . . These illegal devices allow engines to pass EPA's emissions tests in the lab, but turn off pollution control equipment under normal driving conditions—and all to cut a few corners on costs."[36] In October 1998, the diesel engine manufacturers agreed to pay civil penalties totaling $83.4 million; to spend $850 million on producing cleaner engines; to spend $109.5 million on additional environmental projects, such as the development of new emission-control technologies; and to accelerate by 15 months their compliance with new emissions standards. The agency trumpeted the "billion dollar" settlement, but it looks more like an $83.4 million settlement, with the added costs taking the form of expenses the companies would have incurred sooner or later in any event. The penalties were divided according to the numbers of engines produced by each company. Caterpillar and Cummins each paid $25 million while others paid less.

The merits of the case are rather different from what EPA's press releases would lead one to believe.

The current version of the Federal Test Procedure for diesel emissions was promulgated in 1979.[37] The test for gaseous emissions, including nitrogen oxide (NO$_x$), was based on emissions by engines with mechanical carburetors (electronic controls for heavy engines were still in the future) and was designed to measure emissions under urban driving conditions.

This urban focus was based on two factors:

- NO$_x$ is an *urban* problem. It is regulated primarily because it reacts with volatile organic compounds (VOC) to produce ozone, which is one of the six major "criteria pollutants" regulated under the Clean Air Act. Since ozone is exclusively an urban problem, so is NO$_x$.
- According to a recent staff report by the House Committee on Commerce, EPA also calculated that, given mechanical carburetion, controlling NO$_x$ emissions under urban driving conditions would automatically control them under highway, steady-state conditions.[38]

An additional complicating factor is that the importance of NO$_x$ as a pollutant was unclear at the time and remains so to this day. It is far from certain that NO$_x$ reductions gain much in the way of public health improvements.[39]

As engines grew more sophisticated in the 1980s and 1990s, the engine manufacturers had an option that had not existed in 1979. Engines could be programmed to meet the EPA FTP test when operating under urban conditions, but then, in highway driving, recalibrate to increase the level of NO$_x$ emissions in exchange for attaining improved operating performance and fuel economy. The manufacturers took advantage of this possibility. This choice ultimately led to EPA's 1998 action against them for installing "defeat devices."

At the time of the settlement, the manufacturers protested vigorously that EPA had known what they were doing and had acquiesced. The Association of European Vehicle Manufacturers and an expert from the Natural Resources Defense Council agree with the manufacturers.[40] EPA vehemently denied any such knowledge, claiming, "At no time before EPA's discovery of their use in 1997, did any of the engine manufacturers involved in the recent settlement notify EPA of the existence or true nature of the illegal emission control strategies in question."[41]

The staff of the House Commerce Committee probed this episode and put forth overwhelming evidence that EPA was indeed fully informed about manufacturers' actions, with much of the information coming from the manufacturers themselves, starting in 1991.[42] The agency's denials were either the result of internal failures of communication, artful dodges about the meaning of "notify," or simple deceit. However, the House staff report agreed with then EPA administrator Carol Browner's statement that the manufacturers' offense was heinous and, proceeding from this assumption, it then flayed both the companies and the agency for disregarding the public health.

The validity of this assumption is quite dubious, however. Browner may be contemptuous of companies who "want to cut a few corners on costs," but promoting fuel economy, which the recalibrating achieved, is a virtue, according to the U.S. government. Indeed, the government imposes Corporate Average Fuel Economy (CAFE) standards on the automobile industry that result in between 2,600 and 4,500 traffic fatalities each year.[43] Why fuel economy is good when mandated by government, even at such a price in lives, but evil when engaged in by engine manufacturers (at no price in lives, since recalibration does not relate to safety), is not explained by EPA. Nor does EPA demonstrate the slightest interest in whether the economies achieved by the manufacturers' actions provided benefits for consumers in the form of lower prices that exceeded any costs imposed by the increases in NO_x emissions.

In light of these factors and of the uncertainty surrounding the importance of NO_x, it would not be surprising if the EPA Office of Air and Radiation regarded NO_x emissions as a back-burner issue, only to be blindsided by their bosses in 1998.

Browner's characterization of the companies as "cheaters" who were setting out to undermine the Clean Air Act caused significant distrust and bitterness among the manufacturers, who believed they were complying with the regulation and that EPA arbitrarily branded them as violators instead of addressing the underlying issue, which was whether the 1979 FTP test should be changed. The anger was intensified because the manufacturers had little choice but to agree to the settlement. EPA was refusing to certify engines for 1999 until the allegations were settled, so contesting the charge could have put the manufacturers out of business.[44] One manufacturer was quoted as saying that the EPA action "borders on a crime," and that all felt "betrayed." Another commentator observed, "Only a cynic would note that the sensational and surprisingly vitriolic announcements were made about two weeks before the November [1998] elections."[45]

Also, it should be noted, EPA's approach avoids addressing the real question: Does the reduction in NO_x emissions achieved under highway conditions by extending the FTP test in this way justify the costs imposed on consumers? No rulemaking record exists, so we will never know. And that is how EPA prefers it.

6. Retroactive Rulemaking via Evidentiary Standards: The Credible Evidence Rule

In February 1997 EPA adopted a final rule on Credible Evidence for enforcement actions under the Clean Air Act.[1] The rule was developed not by the Air Office but by the Air Enforcement Division of the Office of Regulatory Enforcement of EPA's Office of Enforcement and Compliance Assurance. It is superficially simple, providing that in an enforcement action under the Clean Air Act, a violation can be established not just through one of the specific "Reference Tests" prescribed in EPA's rules but by "any credible evidence" (the rule is called "the ACE rule"). The exact meaning of the term is, deliberately, left undefined. The agency says only that it includes "engineering calculations, indirect estimates of emissions, and direct measurement of emissions by a variety of means." It includes "parametric monitoring" and "continuous emission monitoring." Nothing is excluded, so the scope of the term will be limited only by the bounds of the ingenuity exhibited by EPA and private lawyers in drawing a connection between some fact and a violation of an emissions standard.

Industry challenged the rule, but the action was dismissed as unripe for review by the D.C. Circuit.[2] Thus the validity of the rule will be judged in some future enforcement proceeding.

This rule is a good illustration of EPA's lack of regard for the rule of law. The problem lies not only in the substance of the provision but in the agency's disingenuous responses to comments.

The case against the rule starts with the fact that almost all Clean Air Act rules are technology based. A company is required to install a particular technology that EPA has determined to be adequate and to keep the pollution control equipment in good working order. Formal standards are frequently phrased in terms of emissions limits, but these numbers are derived from the performance characteristics of the favored technology.[3]

57

Almost invariably, going back to the original Clean Air Act of 1970, whenever EPA promulgated an emissions standard for an industry, it also prescribed a reference test for measuring compliance. These tests prescribe the operating conditions under which the pollution control equipment is to be judged and the standards it must meet under these conditions. Clean Air rules contain almost 130 of these reference tests.[4]

As emphasized by Robert Ajax, a longtime and highly respected EPA official in the Air Office, these reference tests are absolutely inseparable from their related numerical emissions limits, in two ways:[5]

First, emissions vary considerably with operating conditions. Because EPA, in its standard-setting process, focuses on the technology to be installed, its interest in the actual emissions level is to ensure that this technology is calibrated properly and is working properly. So EPA established emissions limits based on one set of conditions. If the agency had been required to study all of the possible variations in emissions levels under all of the possible operating conditions, its rulemaking processes would have been interminable.

Second, the emissions limits were established with full awareness that even properly functioning technology would sometimes exceed the emissions limits. Usually, an effort was made to establish the limit at the "95 percent level," meaning that properly functioning technology would meet the level 95 percent of the time. Such a level means that even the most careful industry will be out of compliance 5 percent of the time. However, industry found this level acceptable and acquiesced in the emissions limits, knowing that if the reference test were performed once a year then the industry would exceed the limit only once every 20 years. A risk of one violation and penalty every 20 years was regarded as acceptable, especially if the risk could be reduced still further by ensuring, in advance of the test, that the equipment was indeed functioning properly. However, a 5 percent risk is not acceptable if it means that the industry will be accused of violating the standard 5 percent of the time, which is 18 days each year, and will be subjected to fines of $25,000 per day, plus ritual flagellation in EPA press releases. The affected industries would not have acquiesced in the 95 percent–level standard for setting rules under such circumstances.

One industry representative describes the result:

Numeric emission limits were generally set low enough to compel installation of the "reference controls" on which those limits were based. Facilities were then required to operate and maintain these emission-control measures. . . . But . . . neither EPA nor regulated entities thought this meant *that facilities were additionally required to meet "the number" every minute or hour of the year.* The difference is crucial, because few well-controlled facilities can meet the latter ACE test without having to change their current emission-control strategies. Almost every emitting facility exhibits normal, inherent variability in raw materials, production processes, and control equipment performances. Past emission limits typically *ignored* that long-term variability by setting numbers based on short-term emissions tests. This approach also allowed EPA and states to set many more limits than would have been possible if long-term emissions data had to be collected to show that "the number" would be met by required controls at each covered facility over months or years. But ACE *spotlights* such variability by characterizing as "violations" the 2% or 4% of times these facilities may be over that "number"—even if they're far below it more than 95% of the year. Thus thousands of facilities could be thrown into "violation" on ACE's effective date *despite doing exactly what they were supposed to do*—install and operate reference control measures.[6]

These points were made to the enforcement office during the rulemaking proceeding. EPA cannot claim ignorance. The agency response was to ignore them. The preamble to the final rule simply states that "the number" is an absolute standard that must be met under all circumstances and conditions, a conclusion most definitely not shared by anyone else involved in the process.[7] The agency thus ignores the long history of enforcement under the Clean Air Act, and "redefine[s] in a single rulemaking what constitutes compliance with hundreds of state and federal emission limit regulations that have been promulgated over the past 25 years."[8]

Under the Credible Evidence Rule, industries are now sitting ducks for enforcement actions. Industries collect a great deal of data on their operations and on the performance of their pollution control equipment. These data will often show that emissions are indeed exceeding the level provided for in the standard and allowed under the operating permit. If the standard has been set at the 95 percent level, for example, operating data will show exceedances 5 percent of the time. In the past, these exceedances were not regarded as violations of the standard, because a violation was thought to occur only under the formal circumstances of the reference test. Now, EPA is saying that all exceedances are automatically violations. This not only makes the company liable for heavy penalties, it also makes any individual employee who certified that his company was in compliance with its permit guilty of the criminal malfeasance of false reporting. Intent does not matter, remember, as long as the employee "knowingly" filled out the form.

Consultants to industrial firms report that EPA is now seeking information from the past to find violations of emissions standards from facilities that thought they were in compliance. Potential fines are enormous, considering that each day on which a violation occurs is a separate offense. Also, if an emissions limit is cast in the form of a daily average over a month-long period, then an exceedance of the monthly limit counts not as a single violation but as 30 of them— one for each day of the month.[9]

Such enforcement serves no purpose except vindictiveness and perhaps Ludditism. It does not serve the cause of either compliance or deterrence. Such companies tried to comply and thought they had succeeded. The Credible Evidence Rule is in fact a new law, imposed retroactively, in contravention of people's understanding at the time. It can do nothing for the environment except collect money for EPA. It will only embitter the targets, who are unlikely to be so foolish in the future as to collect any unnecessary data in the interest of improving their environmental performance. As one angry stakeholder put it, "The Credible Evidence Rule exemplifies a new hard-edged, undefined, wide-open, anything-goes enforcement approach."[10]

The problems of those subject to the rule are compounded by the appearance, the year before the Credible Evidence Rule, of EPA's Compliance Assurance Monitoring Rule (CAM), which requires industries to maintain extensive monitoring data on the performance of pollution control equipment.[11] CAM data are a one-way ratchet; bad data can be used to establish a violation of emissions standards, but good data do not provide a shield. The agency can still use any other "credible evidence" to establish a violation. Nor will prompt correction of an exceedance discovered through CAM data provide a defense to an enforcement action, though, of course, at EPA's discretion, it could be presented as a reason to mitigate penalties.

The fate that awaits future alleged violators of the Clean Air Act, if EPA has its way, is foreshadowed by the agency's position in a 1999 administrative case under the Clean Water Act, *City of Salisbury, Maryland*.[12] The city defended against charges that it had disposed of sewage sludge with an excessive concentration of metals by asserting the tests showed that the excesses were laboratory errors and that retesting had shown the concentrations were within legal limits. EPA fought to keep out the additional evidence, asserting that the original tests had to be treated as conclusive. An administrative law judge sided with the city.

7. Legislation through Enforcement

EPA does not limit its lawmaking instincts to expanding the scope of enforcement efforts such as the New Source Review program. It also applies its statutes and regulations to conduct that was not intended to be within the ambit of the law at all. Thus, it engages not only in *regulation* by enforcement but also in *legislation* by enforcement. A variation on the theme is "piling on"—taking an environmental offense that is adequately addressed by one law and bringing a host of other laws to bear on it so as to increase an industry's penalty and/or the EPA's bargaining power.

The prerequisites for expanding either type of regulatory reach include press or public concern and, perhaps, congressional interest in some alleged environmental menace. Of course, the agency is adept at promoting such concern, and the annals of the past 30 years are replete with crises made mostly out of whole cloth.

So many environmental laws now exist, and their elasticity is so great, that ingenuity can find a way to apply them to any new "environmental crisis" that is invented. Following are a few topical examples of EPA's campaign of legislation through regulation. The examples are not meant to be exhaustive; indeed, an entire book could be (and has been) written on the subject.[1] But the fundamental issues can readily be grasped by even a cursory examination of a few cases.

Wetlands Protection

The Refuse Act of 1899 made illegal the deposit of refuse of any sort in the navigable waters of the United States, "whereby navigation shall or may be impeded or obstructed."[2] Notwithstanding the reference to navigation, during the 1960s aggressive government agencies successfully urged activist courts, including the Supreme Court, to turn that law into a general anti-pollution measure, contrary to the understanding of over half a century.[3]

63

After the passage of the Clean Water Act in 1972,[4] a similar train of events occurred in connection with wetlands. EPA and the Army Corps of Engineers, abetted by the courts, took a statute intended to control pollution and turned it into a control on land use, despite the fact that the act barely mentions wetlands and that Congress certainly did not contemplate that it was enacting such a law.[5] These controls are enforced with particular vehemence, perhaps because the agencies realize that their legal and moral foundations are flimsy. As a common practice, the enforcers assert very broad definitions of "wetlands," rely on vagaries of administrative law to keep the accused from challenging regulations in court, and seek criminal penalties against anyone who resists the agency's interpretation of the law.

In 1997, the Fourth Circuit threw out a criminal prosecution on the ground that the wetlands at issue were isolated, unconnected to any interstate waters.[6] In early 2001, the Supreme Court concurred, ruling that federal power does not extend to isolated ponds and rejecting the argument that a mere possibility that a migratory bird might decide to land on a pond provided enough of a hook to interstate commerce to create federal jurisdiction. In reaching its decision, though, the Court made clear that federal power *does* extend to any wetland that *is* connected to other bodies of water.[7]

Before EPA or the Army Corps of Engineers can assert jurisdiction, they must find that the landowner deposited something in a wetland, such as rocks, trash, or chemicals. Precisely because the statute was passed to protect navigation and prevent pollution—and *not* to keep people from draining a wetland—it makes putting materials into water illegal. The statute does not mention removing water from land, or removing material—such as dirt—from a wetland.

Developers quickly realized that statutory provisions against putting materials into water did not keep them from digging drainage ditches and channeling water away, or from taking dirt away from a wetland in the course of digging these ditches. In due time, the water drains off, the wetland ceases to be a wetland, and the development can proceed. And, of course, this activity does not even contradict the purposes of the statute, which were to protect navigation and to prevent pollution of interstate waters, not to serve as a national land-use law. EPA and the Corps were frustrated by this loophole in their administrative code, but instead of going to Congress and asking for a program to buy wetlands, or even to preserve wetlands, they revised their enforcement policy to extend the law even further. They decided that the law against depositing any substance into "waters of the United States" included "fallback," which is dirt that falls off a backhoe while it is being used to dig a ditch. In other words, they claimed that redepositing dirt that had just been dug up, however *de minimis*, was enough to require that the digger seek a permit.

This view was codified in the "Tulloch Rule," which was issued in settlement of an environmentalist lawsuit brought to force EPA and the Corps to deal with the drainage issue.[8] The National Mining Association (NMA) appealed the rule, and the D.C. Circuit decided that the rule exceeded the Corps' authority under the Clean Water Act. "Depositing" a substance could not be defined as including the act of putting some dirt back whence it had just been removed. Regarding the Tulloch Rule the court noted, "Indeed, its overriding purpose appears to be to expand the Corps' permitting authority to encompass incidental fallback, and, as a result, a wide range of activities that cannot remotely be said to 'add' anything to the waters of the United States."[9]

The decision was hailed as a major victory for business (not to mention the rule of law), but such victories have a way of eroding under the assaults of determined enforcers. In 1999, the EPA Board of Environmental Appeals upheld a penalty of $90,000 levied against Slinger Drainage, Inc.[10] Slinger installed drainage tile in a wetland to convert it to farmland. Slinger used a machine that lifted the soil, allowed the tile to be inserted, and immediately redeposited 50 percent of the soil in the ditch. The rest was left momentarily on the side of the ditch, then was pushed by the machine into the ditch to complete the refill. The EPA Board found that Slinger was not protected by the decision in the National Mining Association's case because Slinger redeposited *all* of the dirt it removed, not just some of it. In other words, Slinger made *less* of a change in the land, but in doing so it provided EPA with a jurisdictional hook on which to hang the company.

Oil Spills

Oil spills are subject to a comprehensive regulatory scheme under the Oil Pollution Act (OPA) of 1990, which amended the Clean Water Act. EPA is not content to rely on this law to govern oil spills because that would force the agency to pay attention to the OPA's complicated balancing of the need to protect the environment against the realities of an energy-dependent society. EPA has found that, with creative enforcement practices, far harsher penalties are available under other parts of the Clean Water Act; the Comprehensive Environmental Response, Compensation, and Liability Act; the Resource Conservation and Recovery Act; the Refuse Act; the Act to Prevent Pollution from Ships; the Ocean Dumping Act; and even the Migratory Bird Treaty Act. In one oil spill case, even though no human harm occurred, the government charged a company with a criminal violation of the prohibition against sending an unseaworthy vessel to sea when it was likely to endanger the life of an individual.[11]

This sort of piling on is exceedingly common. Sometimes, of course, it can be justified. Congress may pass one statute knowing that other laws already cover the same conduct, and wanting to multiply the protections. Often, though, regulatory agencies simply decide that certain conduct should be punished more heavily than Congress has provided for directly, stretching a different statute to achieve this end. Often, multiplying counts in an indictment is also a useful bargaining ploy. The more a defendant can be charged with, the greater his total exposure and the more he will have to pay to settle. Multiple counts also make defendants amenable to funding Special Environmental Projects.

Urban and Suburban Development

A current hot environmental issue is urban/suburban sprawl. In 1999, the head of EPA's Region I said that the agency has an "unwavering commitment to use the full force of environmental law to oppose ... those projects which—by their very nature— contribute to sprawl."[12] This statement is no empty threat. The Clean Air Act and the Clean Water Act present the most obvious handles, but there are a host of others. Any statute that requires EPA to issue permits leaves enough discretion in the hands of the agency to enable it to block growth by delay alone if it so wishes.

EPA also uses its grant authority to fight sprawl. Over a period of five years, EPA's Transportation Partner Program gave grants of more than $6 million to nine environmental groups, which then passed the money on to local anti-road groups.[13]

EPA is also becoming heavily engaged in the "Environmental Justice" movement, which discourages investment and industrial development in minority areas. The Environmental Justice program purports to be based on the need to keep minorities from bearing a disproportionate burden of exposure to pollution. In fact, it is based on the dislike that EPA and its environmentalist constituency bear for industrial development. Facts supporting the premise that minority neighborhoods suffer more from pollution than others simply do not exist, and the premise that minority communities are better off without the employment generated by modern facilities is absurd.[14]

Superfund enforcement also affects urban growth patterns. The financial exposure of becoming involved in a Superfund site can be ruinous. As a result, sensible corporate managers refuse to consider locating a new facility on an existing industrial site. They insist on a pristine location where they cannot possibly be subjected to EPA's Superfund liability rules. At the same time, EPA is spending millions of dollars in grants designed to promote investment in "brownfields."

Biotechnology and EPA

The debate over biotechnology offers a grand opportunity for regulatory expansion. People are concerned and, because most people have little understanding of the topic, sparks of public anxiety can easily be fanned into flames of fear.

For example, consider EPA's campaign against frost-resistant genes. Snow-making machinery uses proteins derived from bacteria known as "ice-plus," which serve as nuclei for frost formation. Spontaneous mutations, however, can keep the protein from being made. Scientists thus created a strain, called "ice-minus," that mimics the frost-inhibiting properties of the mutant strain, a useful invention for farmers. When the agriculture industry introduced the strain into crops as a means of preventing frost damage, the EPA declared that the frost-resistant genes were a "pest," and that ice-minus is therefore subject to regulation under the Federal Insecticide, Fungicide, and Rodenticide Act (FIFRA). Ultimately, after extensive and expensive tests, EPA decided that ice-minus was all right. In the meantime, scientist Michael Gough notes, "millions of people saw newspaper and television coverage of farm workers forced to wear moonsuits and breathe through respirators while spraying the completely innocuous bacteria."[15] More important, however, the precedent was set: bioengineered genes can be defined as pests or pesticides under FIFRA, and regulated accordingly.

8. Federal-State Relations

Many environmental laws split responsibility between EPA and the states. Under the Clean Air Act, for example, most authority over stationary sources has been delegated to the states. Under the Resource Conservation and Recovery Act, a state develops a plan, and if it is satisfactory, EPA then delegates authority over the program to the state.

Many states have a more sophisticated attitude than EPA. They recognize that improving the environment is a long-term commitment, a marathon rather than a sprint. They emphasize compliance rather than enforcement and do not assume that all violations are the result of evil intent or lack of environmental consciousness. They encourage companies to fix problems on their own, perhaps quietly, even if their action deprives the government of penalties and politically useful ends. Becky Norton Dunlop, secretary of natural resources in Virginia during the 1990s, expressed this perspective when she said, "Enforcement action means 'failure,' not success. It is certainly not the best tool to improve the quality and condition of the resources which make up our environment. In fact, it is the tool of last resort."[1] Dunlop also summed up her view of EPA in the subtitle of her recent book, *Clearing the Air: How the People of Virginia Improved the State's Air and Water Despite the EPA.*[2]

EPA's attitude toward such a belief resembles the horror that might strike a 16th-century church inquisitor upon meeting a modern-day Unitarian. It is heresy, and grounds for excommunication or worse. EPA and the states consequently wage constant battles over audit policy and other compliance-oriented efforts that seem, to EPA, to represent a retreat from an enforcement mindset.

This section briefly reviews several typical battles over enforcement policies.

U.S. v. Smithfield Foods

EPA's hostility toward Virginia during Dunlop's tenure was palpable, due partly to differences in approach and partly to partisan political differences. The Democratic federal administration could not have it be thought that a Republican state government might actually take effective action to protect the environment by following a philosophy different from EPA's. In testimony before a congressional committee, and in her more recent book, Dunlop recounted a long string of insults, violations of agreements, and rhetorical attacks.[3]

The hostility led to the infamous *Smithfield* case.[4] Smithfield Foods was and is both a significant employer in Virginia and a significant source of phosphorous and nitrogen discharges into the Pagan River. In 1988, EPA lowered allowable levels of phosphorous. Smithfield sued, arguing that the new standard could not be met with current technology, and was thus not authorized by the statute. In 1991, the company and the state, then under a Democratic administration, entered a consent agreement to resolve both the suit and the underlying problem. Smithfield dropped its challenge to the rule and the state allowed it to continue to discharge in excess of the limits while a new sewer line was being built to carry its waste to a treatment plant 17 miles away. The company put up several million dollars to help build the line, and in 1997 the discharges into the river ceased.

Unfortunately, the actual discharge levels were not reflected in the renewal of Smithfield's discharge permit, issued in 1992, after the consent agreement was made (permits are "administered" by the state but "overseen" by EPA, in the words of the appellate court). Nor did the company formally request modifications of its consent agreement when construction of the sewer line was delayed beyond the expected completion date in 1994. These derelictions gave EPA an opening, and in December 1996 it filed suit seeking penalties for the effluent limit violations. The suit also asserted that the company and one of its employees had engaged in false reporting and destruction of records.

EPA won on summary judgment, and the company was fined $12.6 million, a verdict upheld on appeal. This judgment could be called a victory of sorts by Smithfield; EPA had asked for penalties of $125 million. The operator of the wastewater treatment plants pled guilty to both illegal discharges and false reporting, and went to jail for 30 months.[5]

The Department of Justice asserted that federal action was necessary because "despite the seriousness of Smithfield's violations, the

Commonwealth was taking no action to assess penalties. . . . Rather, in the face of threats by the [company] to leave the Commonwealth, . . . Virginia entered into a series of agreements."⁶ Dunlop views it rather differently. She noted that EPA had "known and acquiesced in the results-driven actions Virginia has taken [on the matter] since 1991," that Virginia had been on the verge of taking civil action against Smithfield to hurry up the process but was asked to defer while EPA investigated criminally, and that EPA had made false, rhetorical statements about the state and its actions.⁷

EPA may just have been engaging in headhunting behavior. However, the timing looks political. In Virginia, the state attorney general is responsible for environmental enforcement. At the time the suit was brought, the Republican attorney general was running for governor, and the Democrats hoped to profit by tagging him as soft on environmental enforcement.⁸

Harmon Industries v. EPA

Harmon Industries became a cause célèbre among business owners and environmental lawyers, a poster child for EPA's heavy-handed indifference to both true environmental protection and the rule of law.⁹ In the words of Harmon's chairman, the "case well illustrates the way in which conscientious regulated industries who are seeking in good faith to comply with their obligations under the environmental laws can be whipsawed by EPA's claimed 'overfiling' authority."¹⁰

Harmon operated a circuit-board assembly plant. Employees used solvents, and from 1973 to 1987 the employees disposed of the residues by tossing them out the back door onto the ground. About 30 gallons per month were disposed of in this manner. Management was unaware of this practice, assuming that the solvents were used until depleted and that any residues evaporated. In November 1987, management learned of it during an environmental compliance audit.

The company promptly stopped the practice and became the first in the industry to switch to a manufacturing process that used non-hazardous cleaning material, at an initial cost of $800,000 and an annual cost of $125,000. It also hired a consultant to investigate the effect of the prior disposal on soil and groundwater, and in May 1988 it received a report that several hazardous chemicals were present in the soil but not at levels that presented a danger to human health or the environment. In June, Harmon took the report to the Missouri Department of Natural Resources (MDNR)—which administers the Resource Conservation and Recovery Act in the state—and each subsequent step was overseen by MDNR. EPA also saw some of Harmon's reports, but it denies receiving all of them.

Harmon commissioned further analysis and in 1992 gave MDNR a consultant's report concluding that the remaining solvent did not pose a threat due to the lack of exposure pathways. Harmon gave a closure report to MDNR recounting the decision to leave the material in place, and MDNR gave Harmon a post-closure permit in 1996.[11] The investigation cost Harmon $1.4 million, and additional costs of $500,000 for a 30-year post-closure period were anticipated.

Starting in 1991, Harmon and MDNR began negotiations over Harmon's offense, and in 1993 the two filed with a court a complaint and consent decree. The decree imposed no monetary penalties against Harmon and stated that it settled matters between the state and the company.

In the meantime, as early as 1990, EPA's Region VII wrote to MDNR saying that Harmon should pay penalties. EPA threatened to initiate its own enforcement action if the state failed to heed this demand. That threat was executed in 1991, before the final state consent decree, when EPA filed an administrative complaint seeking penalties of almost $2.8 million. In 1994, an EPA administrative law judge assessed a penalty of $586,716, a decision upheld in the EPA internal review process. In 1997, Harmon challenged the penalty in the U.S. District Court.

From an environmental practitioner's perspective, *Harmon* presents important questions concerning legal relationships between EPA and the states and the authority of EPA to "overfile" when a state is already acting. On these issues, the trial court found for Harmon; it decided that the terms of the RCRA provide that once a state has been delegated the authority to administer the statute, EPA can bring an enforcement action only if it notifies the state of a violation and the state fails to act, or if it withdraws the state's authority. EPA objected to the decision, appealed the matter to the Eighth Circuit, and lost.

Legal issues aside, however, no aspect of EPA's conduct makes good sense. Tossing used solvent out the back door was a common practice in many industries. The RCRA, passed in 1976 and strengthened in 1986, has been interpreted to require an end to this practice.

Perhaps Harmon was a little slow in adopting the new environmental ethic, but this dereliction caused no harm, and once company management became aware of the problem it acted responsibly, swiftly, and at considerable expense. It also adopted an aggressive pollution prevention scheme, again at considerable expense.

Furthermore, the MDNR appears to have dealt with the matter perfectly appropriately. It said, more or less, "Thanks for telling us, change the practice, make sure the stuff doesn't do any harm, and we'll call it quits." EPA, on the other hand, appears to have acted with pointless malice. Its position would punish a company for coming forward voluntarily, and it encourages recalcitrance. Had EPA won the appeal, it would also have undermined the administration of the RCRA by making it impossible for a company to know with whom to negotiate or how to reach closure on an issue.

Moreover, EPA stretched the statute to maximize the company's potential liability and sought a penalty out of proportion to the damage caused or to the gravity of the offense. The complaint charged Harmon with operating a hazardous waste landfill without a permit and with failing to register as a hazardous waste generator, and characterized the offense as "very serious." The first of the charges is bogus. Had Harmon known of its employees' practice, it would not have gone into the business of operating a hazardous waste disposal site; it would have called a disposal company to haul the stuff away. The failure to register might be valid, but the quantities might also be small enough to have allowed Harmon to escape the registration requirement as a small quantity generator. The only honest charge would have been that Harmon disposed of hazardous waste improperly.

By multiplying the charges, EPA could raise the penalties sought to a total of $2,777,324. (The administrative law judge granted penalties of $587,716.) The first factor in the model used by EPA in calculating penalties is costs avoided by noncompliance with the law. In Harmon's case, the *real* avoided costs were about $6,000—what proper disposal would have cost. By classifying Harmon as a hazardous waste disposal site, EPA could count as "costs avoided" all of the costs that would normally be incurred in such an enterprise, such as liners, insurance, continuing monitoring, and so on. Running a hazardous waste disposal business is expensive. The requested penalties were then raised further by an EPA finding that the violations had "an extremely high potential for harm" despite the lack of any actual harm, despite the lack of any pathway for human exposure, and despite the fact that "during the administrative proceedings EPA presented no evidence to dispute the conclusion that the limited contamination . . . presented no significant threat to human health or the environment. The testimony showed that EPA personnel had not read the studies conducted by either Harmon or MDNR."[12]

Environmental Audits

Another area of state and federal conflict, audit policy, is not described in detail here because so much has already been written about it over the past few years.[13] States repeatedly try to install rules to encourage companies to search for and correct environmental problems and violations. In pursuit of this goal, states are willing to be lenient with respect to penalties. Missouri's attitude in *Harmon* is typical. EPA is vehemently opposed to such leniency, insisting that penalties should be imposed no matter what. To combat state resistance, EPA threatens to target companies in states that enact audit amnesties and to pummel states into accepting its heavy-handed enforcement practices. As two experts commented, in 1998, "In spite of an utter lack of credible evidence that these audit protections have been used improperly to shield wrongdoers from deserved liability . . . EPA, joined by the Department of Justice (DOJ) has initiated an increasingly aggressive campaign to eliminate state audit laws."[14]

A classic example of the issues surrounding the environmental audit debate is the experience of Coors Brewing Company.

First, some background. EPA often estimates rather than measures emissions from industrial facilities. It does this by making calculations about likely levels on the basis of the type of operation, what is known about the substances used, and, perhaps, some sample measurements. Then EPA allows companies to use these estimates as substitutes for actual measurements.

In 1992, EPA followed this practice in estimating emissions from breweries. Coors performed a voluntary internal audit and found that EPA's estimated figures were only 10 percent of the actual emissions. So Coors reported this result to state authorities and the EPA. EPA, instead of thanking the company, promptly fined it $1 million for violating the Clean Air Act.[15]

In recent times, EPA has given ground somewhat on audits. It has agreed to impose penalties based only on the economic gains derived from the offense, waiving penalties based on the "gravity" of the offense if nine specific conditions are met.[16] Given the agency's math concerning the alleged economic gains in *Harmon*, however, this may not always mean much. Nor is it clear that Coors would have been protected by the latest policy. One of EPA's conditions is that the problem be discovered through a "systematic" audit process. If a company finds a problem through a special inquiry or by accident, it does not count. Furthermore, EPA remains adamantly opposed to any formal "audit privilege" that would shield audit reports from government scrutiny. EPA says it will not "routinely" ask for audit reports, but this seems like a meaningless promise. It means only that EPA will not go fishing unless it wants to.

The states are also standing their ground. Creative environmental policies are taking root there, based on compliance models, not enforcement models, and the states are increasingly convinced that their approach is the right one for the long term.[17]

9. Civil Liberties and Constitutional Rights

In 1995, Timothy Lynch of the Cato Institute published *Polluting Our Principles: Environmental Prosecutions and the Bill of Rights*.[1] One of the study's main topics was discussed earlier—diluting the requirement of intent in the context of environmental enforcement. The study also documents the extent to which businesses subject to environmental laws cannot rely on the fundamental protections of the Bill of Rights. For instance,

- *Searches and Seizures.* Many environmental laws provide for warrantless searches, making refusing entry to the inspectors a criminal offense. The Supreme Court has held that commercial property is largely outside of the protection of the Fourth Amendment against unreasonable or warrantless searches, especially when the premises involve "closely regulated" industries. Considering the broad coverage of environmental regulation, it is difficult to think of any business that could not be classified as "closely regulated."

- *Double Jeopardy.* The courts have long held to the "dual sovereignty" interpretation of the Fifth Amendment's bar on multiple prosecutions for the same offense. Under this theory, the safeguard is only against a second prosecution by the same sovereign. Because the federal government and a state government are different sovereigns, an action by one, successful or not, does not bar an action by the other on the basis of the same facts. Environmental regulation is rife with parallel federal and state structures, thus creating the possibility of double jeopardy for almost any alleged offense.

- *Self-Incrimination.* In 1906, the Supreme Court held that corporate officers cannot invoke the privilege against self-incrimination on behalf of their employers. Companies are required to provide mountains of data. If any of the data establish that an emissions limit has been exceeded, then the government automatically has made a criminal case, given the irrelevance of intent. Nor do employees have any privilege against self-incrimination if ordered to produce business records that might incriminate them personally. The exposure goes beyond the production of existing records. Under the Toxic Substances Control Act, EPA can subpoena "answers to questions," thereby using the subpoena, in effect, to compel testimony.

Since Lynch's publication, the federal government's stance on such matters has toughened, especially on environmental matters, and especially where corporations are involved. The attorney-client privilege is under attack. Defense lawyers say prosecutors are insisting as a condition of settlement that business defendants and their lawyers waive attorney-client and work-product privileges, and the problem has grown severe enough to trigger a letter from the American Corporate Counsel Association to the deputy attorney general. DOJ denies any such policy, a statement that, according to defense lawyers, "belies the truth."[2]

On other occasions, DOJ insists that such a requirement is reasonable because a company will often blame environmental infractions on employees who, according to the company, violated policy. The government, it argues, needs to inquire into the validity of the claim. However, such a demand is also part of a general government strategy of pitting companies and their employees against each other.

Two civil liberties attorneys recently pointed out that the hardball prosecutorial tactics used by the independent counsel's office, and objected to by many in the press, are in fact the standard tactics of prosecutors.[3] The basic game is called "flipping"—prosecutors catch a lower-level functionary in a legal violation and inform him that he is going to jail unless he gives the prosecutors someone higher up in the company. It is indeed a way of finding violators at the top of the organizational pyramid. It is also a way of inducing perjury, since the low-level official who refuses to testify against his superior will face heavy penalties. And under the sentencing guidelines, his term will be increased for his "failure to cooperate."

This game can be played with particular success in the environmental area, given the number and intricacy of the laws, the irrelevance of intent, and the multiplication of the penalties by use of the "separate violation" principles. The potential exposure and the staggering costs of mounting a defense are enough to ruin anyone who is not exceedingly wealthy, and the temptation to cooperate with the prosecutors is overwhelming. In the *Hanousek* case, for example, much of the evidence against the defendant was supplied by the forklift operator who had actually made the mistake that caused the damage.

A recent case demonstrating EPA's fundamental lack of regard for civil liberties in environmental enforcement is *United States v. Omega Chemical Corp.*[4] Omega was the target of a criminal investigation concerning importation of chlorofluorocarbons (CFC). It also operated a solvent recycling facility that, in EPA's judgment, presented a threat of a release of hazardous substances. Upon being informed that Omega lacked the financial resources to implement the remedial work required by EPA, the agency assumed primary responsibility for removal actions.

The agency asked Omega to sign a consent decree allowing unconditional access to the site. The draft letter contained the following language: "This written permission is given by me voluntarily with knowledge of my right to refuse and without threats or promises of any kind." It is not clear whether Omega signed this initial consent.

Thereafter, EPA prepared an order containing its response plan and directed compliance by Omega. Omega did not object to the substance of the plan, but wrote to EPA that it would not "consent" to access in that it would not waive any objections with respect to unconsented-to searches under the Fourth Amendment. It would, however, cooperate with the remedial effort and would grant physical access. The company further acknowledged EPA's legal authority to come onto the property to alleviate an environmental danger.

EPA then obtained an administrative warrant for access to the property. It also executed various criminal search warrants in connection with the CFC matter and brought a judicial civil penalty action against Omega, asking for $2,500 per day for denial of access for a period of 78 days, even though uncontradicted evidence showed that EPA was in fact on site and performing the remedial work during the entire period. The trial court assessed a penalty of $195,000.

On appeal, the court ruled that EPA exceeded its legal authority. The relevant statute granted the agency a right of access, but nothing authorized EPA to require unconditional consent as long as this physical access was unimpeded. Penalties can be assessed against someone who "unreasonably" denies access, but this does not mean that someone who fails to grant unconditional written consent can be penalized. The court noted the "paradoxical" nature of EPA's insistence that Omega must, on pain of heavy penalties, sign a consent stating explicitly that no threats had been made about what would happen if the company failed to sign.

10. Avenues for Reform

Imposing a proper respect for the rule of law on environmental enforcement is a formidable task. There is no clear path or easy prescription.

The Blind Alley of Incremental Reform

It is tempting to place the entire blame on the Clinton administration's leadership of EPA and the Department of Justice. Certainly, these agencies under the Clinton administration greatly exacerbated the problem. The New Source Review controversy, the Credible Evidence Rule, the automobile cases, and the political demonization perpetrated by one-sided press releases stand as examples.

However, current problems represent only the latest developments of a breakdown in the rule of law that started long before the current leaders took office. Legal doctrines diluting the requirement of intent, rejecting the need for fair notice, or deferring to agency interpretations that expand the agency's own authority were created long before the 1990s, and their creation opened the door to current problems.[1] "Failures of environmental regulation . . . do not occur randomly or . . . as a result of bad management. . . . Rather, they stem from deep-rooted institutional and political incentives that systematically bias the EPA's decisions."[2] A significant purpose of the rule of law is to protect against official abuses, because everyone knows that officials with a propensity for abuse do indeed appear from time to time. Failure to adhere to ancient wisdom left us vulnerable.

Furthermore, the actions of the last administration represent only the extreme example of a trend that was already in existence. Protests against EPA's aggrandizing tendencies have been rife for 25 years, since the mid-1970s.[3] Throughout this period, bills have been introduced to mandate impact statements, risk assessments, congressional review of rules, or other procedural hoops for EPA to jump through. Some of these bills have actually been enacted, either by

Congress or through Executive Order, but the impact, if any, has been small. Requirements that are not enforced by courts or by the Office of Management and Budget might as well not exist.[4] For example, although Executive Order 12612 on Federalism Impact was promulgated in 1987, a recent General Accounting Office study of EPA rules found that the agency did not mention the Order in any of the 1,914 final rules it issued between April 1996 and December 1998.[5]

For 25 years EPA and its partisans have resisted change. It is not that they oppose reform, they say, but that it is no longer necessary. They keep giving the same speeches and writing the same articles, reassuring us that EPA was once mean but is now mellow. It once believed in command-and-control but is now devoted to markets. It now understands that concentration on hard-nosed enforcement is shortsighted, and it plans to foster compliance. For example, a talk given in June 2000 by EPA's deputy administrator makes all of these points, just as all of his predecessors made them.[6] The reality behind the rhetoric, however, consists of the problems described in this paper, and speeches about earnest dedication to markets and the rule of law turn into black humor.

It should surprise no one that 25 years of talk about regulatory reform has achieved little. The vague language of the federal environmental statutes and the corresponding massive delegation of authority to EPA to make law, enforce law, and adjudicate violations concentrate tremendous power in the hands of the agency, breeding insensitivity, zealotry, and abuse. Experience has shown that regulatory agencies will tend to expand until checked, and the potential for regulatory expansion at the EPA, unbounded as it is by congressional language, is vast. Moreover, EPA, like any government agency, is a political organism. Most people are rationally ignorant of the complexities of these issues and cases, and, hearing only the agency's side, are easily convinced that they are being protected. Heavy-handed enforcement seems to satisfy much of the public.

EPA has had and still has many good and honest staff members, interested in protecting the environment without causing undue harm to EPA's regulated communities. Unfortunately, those are rarely the ones calling the enforcement shots. As EPA staff members say, though not for attribution, "They have been put into dry desk."

EPA as an institution appears uninterested in regulatory reform. Both industry and academic commentators regularly assume that if only they explain, once more, the basic principles of risk assessment, the concept of *de minimis* risk, the injustice of a lack of fair notice, or the inevitability of making tradeoffs among different good things, such as wealth creation and environmental protection, then *this time* EPA will understand, will not treat those in the business of produc- ing energy or chemicals or other economic goods as evildoers, and will revamp its policies. Environmental libraries are full of reports, studies, and analyses, almost all of which have had no impact whatsoever.[7]

So, although installing leaders dedicated to the rule of law would be of great help, that alone is not sufficient. Measures are needed that will prevent similar abuses from occurring in the future.

Inside vs. Outside Reform

When American governmental institutions fail to control them- selves, we rely on the oversight responsibilities or regulatory author- ities of other institutions to control them. Much of the problem with EPA is due to the failure of these other institutions—the White House, Congress, the courts, the press. If things are to change, the context within which EPA operates must be changed.

A crucial first step is to recognize the problem: EPA is an agency that has as its sole mission the task of protecting the environment, and it cannot be relied on to be an arbiter of collisions between this value and other values, such as promotion of higher living standards and innovation, survival of small businesses, or respecting prop- erty rights.

Judicial, executive, legislative, and public deference to an agency's choices in making such tradeoffs is based on an antiquated premise about the structure of government that is sometimes called the "transmission belt theory" of administrative law.[8] According to this view, legislators pass laws to promote the public interest. Dedicated regulators then mull over these mandates, bringing disinterested expertise to bear on the execution of the legislative will. Interpreta- tions in this model are interstitial, filling in the gaps of the legisla- tors' intent.

The only people who believe in this transmission belt model any longer are in the legal profession—primarily judges and law profes- sors—who are committed to it as a matter of abstract legal theory. Everyone else, including practicing lawyers, works in a different and more sophisticated reality in which the bromides of the civics books are trumped by the insights of public choice theory and the teachings of practical experience.

Legislators are not primarily concerned with the public interest. They are complicated political animals concerned about many things, including, of course, reelection. Agencies are not staffed by disinterested public servants but by normal human beings, who comprise the usual mix of the energetic and the slothful, the virtuous and the venal, the time-servers and the ideologues, the intelligent and the stupid. They serve their own interests, the public interest, and the interests of their significant reference groups in varying proportions.[9]

EPA operates in this real world of personal and political goal seeking, not in the magical kingdom of administrative law theory. It takes advantage of its power to interpret laws and regulations in the course of enforcement proceedings as a vehicle for imposing new and stricter interpretations of the environmental laws. EPA's interpretations are not interstitial filling-in-the-gaps of legislative intent but the imposition of requirements that were not considered by Congress or anticipated by the affected industries at the time of passage.

The regulated community and the public policy community (such as think tanks and public interest law firms) should conduct aggressive defenses in the courts and educational efforts in the Congress and the executive branch to reveal the defects of the transmission belt theory and the legal doctrines that derive from it.[10] In particular, they should promote elimination of the doctrine that an agency can interpret rules in the context of enforcement proceedings (except perhaps in minor ways) and promote a Fair Notice requirement.

Unfortunately, legal advocacy has proven deficient in these areas so far. Because of the incentives for lawyers to focus on the immediate case, they are forced, in any given instance, to accept the assumptions underlying the transmission belt theory even when every knowledgeable person knows they are nonsense. Advocates need to drop this pretense and be willing to tell the truth. In the early part of this century, the "Brandeis Brief" became famous, as advocate Louis Brandeis forced the courts to look at the realities of industrial society instead of legal abstractions. An analogous effort is called for here. Judges must be encouraged—indeed, forced—to analyze cases in terms of the realities of the administrative state, not the legal abstractions of academic doctrines.

The *Chevron* Doctrine

A recent Supreme Court case creates new hope that the Court is indeed beginning to recast its thinking into a more modern mode. In an important recent opinion that produced absolutely no media comment, the Court cut back on an important legal doctrine known as *Chevron*.

Ever since the creation of the administrative state, courts have adopted the position that agencies have expertise in their areas of responsibility—that is, after all, why Congress created them—and that this expertise extends to problems of interpreting the meaning of the laws establishing the agency. Until 1984, however, the Supreme Court took the position that statutory interpretation was, in the end, a legal question and, thus, the ultimate responsibility lay with the judges. A court would listen to an agency as a kind of super-expert entitled to great deference, but it was not bound by its views. A typical statement from 1968 follows:

> The construction put on a statute by the agency charged with administering it is entitled to deference by the courts, and ordinarily that construction will be affirmed if it has a "reasonable basis in law.". . . But the courts are the final authorities on issues of statutory construction, . . . and "are not obliged to stand aside and rubber-stamp their affirmance of administrative decisions that they deem inconsistent with a statutory mandate or that frustrate the congressional policy underlying a statute." . . . "The deference owed to an expert tribunal cannot be allowed to slip into a judicial inertia."[11]

In 1984, the Supreme Court radically shifted this balance of power in *Chevron U.S.A. v. Natural Resources Defense Council*.[12] There, the Court said that the interpretation of ambiguous statutes is primarily a function of the agencies, not the courts. If a reviewing court, using the conventional tools of legislative interpretation, finds that the meaning of a law is clear, then the court will impose that interpretation. If, however, the court finds that the law is unclear, that Congress did not have an intent with respect to the precise point at issue, then it will defer to any agency interpretation that is within the bounds of reasonableness. The court cannot impose its own views.

An analogous legal doctrine gave agencies equal or even greater authority in the interpretation of their own rules. In *Seminole Rock*, which predated *Chevron* by almost 40 years, the Supreme Court said,

> Since this case involves an interpretation of an administrative regulation a court must necessarily look to the administrative construction of the regulation if the meaning of the words used is in doubt. The intention of Congress or the principles of the Constitution in some situations may be relevant in the first instance in choosing between various constructions. But the ultimate criterion is the administrative interpretation, which becomes of controlling weight unless it is plainly erroneous or inconsistent with the regulation.[13]

The *Seminole Rock* doctrine creates an incentive for agencies to write ambiguous regulations. As noted by Professor John Manning,

> If an agency's rules mean whatever it says they mean (unless that reading is plainly erroneous), the agency effectively has the power of self-interpretation. This authority permits an agency to supply the meaning of regulatory gaps or ambiguities of its own making and relieves the agency of the cost of the imprecision that it has produced. This state of affairs makes it much less likely that an agency will give clear notice of its policies either to those who participated in the rulemaking process prescribed by the Administrative Procedures Act (APA) or to the regulated public.[14]

Daniel Troy of the American Enterprise Institute has spelled out the implications for agency behavior:

> If agencies get deference in the interpretation of their own ambiguous regulations, creating such ambiguity enables them to preserve their own flexibility (and power) to address unanticipated future situations. After all, only prophets, and not bureaucrats, can foretell the future. Writing ambiguous rules enables them to avoid making hard choices at the time of the rulemaking. Ambiguity reduces their political and monetary costs. Instead, regulators can wait until they find an actor that they deem sufficiently "bad" to warrant action, apply the ambiguous regulation to that actor, and claim deference to their own interpretation. The risk of ambiguity is borne entirely by those regulated, and not at all by the agency. As Professor Manning put it, "under *Seminole Rock*, an agency can safely select words having 'so little color of their own that they can be made to take almost any hue.'"[15]

Similarly, the Chevron doctrine has the same effect on legislation. Agencies have a strong role in drafting laws, and Chevron encourages them to encourage Congress to maximize delegation and ambiguity.

Many of the problems discussed in this analysis—fair notice, the New Source Review and automobile litigations, the Credible Evidence Rule—are in large part *Chevron* or *Seminole Rock* decision problems. EPA is relying on its power to make the law in the course of enforcement actions.

Recently, however, the courts have been growing uneasy over the agencies' use of *Chevron*. In *Sutton v. United Airlines*,[16] the Supreme Court decided that the Americans with Disabilities Act does not cover people who need glasses. It reached its decision on the basis that the meaning of the law was clear, and thus a court had no obligation to give *Chevron*-based deference to the contrary interpretations of the administering agencies. However, three different agencies and eight of nine courts of appeal had come out the opposite way, which makes the idea that the meaning was plain rather ridiculous.[17]

In *FDA v. Brown and Williamson Tobacco Co.*,[18] the Supreme Court rejected the FDA's assertion of authority to regulate tobacco products. The Court restated the *Chevron* standard, but went on to hold that the meaning of the statute is clear and contrary to that adopted by the agency. But in reaching this conclusion it considered not just the immediate language of the law but "the statutory context," the need to interpret the law "as a symmetrical and coherent regulatory scheme," the impact of other statutes "to the topic at hand," and "common sense as to the manner in which Congress is likely to delegate a policy decision of such economic and political magnitude to an administrative agency."

All of this language sounds rather un-*Chevron*-like, and a month later the Court explicitly cut back on an important element of the *Chevron* doctrine. The problem that spawned the change was that it had never been clear exactly how far judicial deference was supposed to extend. That is, was a court forced to defer only to an interpretation issued by an agency after formal processes, such as notice-and-comment rulemaking, or was an off-the-cuff decision by a lower-level bureaucrat enough to bind the U.S. Supreme Court?[19]

In *Christensen v. Harris County*, a party relied on an interpretation of a federal law contained in an opinion letter written by the acting administrator of a subdivision of the Department of Labor. A majority of the Supreme Court declined to defer to the Department of Labor, saying, "Interpretations . . . in opinion letters—like interpretations contained in policy statements, agency manuals, and enforcement guidelines, all of which lack the force of law—do not warrant *Chevron*-style deference."[20]

This statement is an important change in the power of agencies. However, the Court will still defer to interpretations adopted through formal rulemaking processes, and the majority was shaky. Only five votes upheld this limitation on the scope of *Chevron*. Justice Scalia regarded the fact that the interpretation was endorsed in a brief filed in the Court as sufficient indication that it constituted the position of the Secretary of Labor to entitle it to *Chevron* deference. However, he concurred in the judgment on the ground that this was not a reasonable reading of the statute.[21]

This is an important, if tenuous, victory for good sense. The pre-*Chevron* rule was a more realistic reflection of the realities of the situation. Of course, courts need the views of administrators on legal issues—and these views should be considered carefully—but granting agencies untrammeled power was a mistake, especially when an agency shows itself willing to delegate further—down to, for example, enforcement officials—who do not embody substantive expertise. No agency should be given carte blanche to define the extent of its own mandate.

In *United States v. Mead Corp.*, decided on June 18, 2001, the Supreme Court limited *Chevron* still further. It said, "We hold that administrative implementation of a particular statutory provision qualifies for *Chevron* deference when it appears that Congress delegated authority to the agency generally to make rules carrying the force of law, and that the agency interpretation claiming deference was promulgated in the exercise of that authority. Delegation of such authority may be shown in a variety of ways, as by an agency's power to engage in adjudication or notice-and-comment rulemaking, or by some other indication of a comparable congressional intent."

That decision leaves unclear the status of interpretations issued in enforcement actions, guidance documents, and other interpretations that are made in the course of programs that are administered through rules.

The Nondelegation Doctrine

The best way of reintroducing vigor to the nondelegation doctrine is to adopt the Congressional Responsibility Act sponsored by Rep. J. D. Hayworth (R-Ariz.) and 54 co-sponsors in the House (H.R. 105) and Sen. Sam Brownback (R-Kans.) and 8 co-sponsors in the Senate (S. 908). The bills would generally require that any regulatory proposal that institutes a new set of requirements on the regulated community be affirmatively adopted by both the House and Senate and signed into law by the president before it could be enforced by regulatory agencies. Essentially, these proposed bills would ensure that elected representatives, not unelected bureaucrats or enforcement officials, have the final say over the law of the land.

Piecemeal Reform

The problems surrounding intent need to be addressed systematically. Criminal charges should be reserved for cases in which the law was clear, known, and flouted, or in which a defendant acted with recklessness in the safety of others. Other matters can be adequately handled by civil penalties. If EPA will not reform itself, then public interest organizations should draft a model bill. This should also encompass the problems identified in Lynch's work concerning the many ways in which environmental defendants' civil rights have been abolished.

Enforcement should also devolve to the states. The states are better at reflecting the preferences of local communities regarding environmental protection and wealth creation and at properly assessing the best schedule for reducing pollution in existing plants. Environmentalists hate this, claiming that states are in the pocket of industry. This may sometimes be true, but on the other hand environmentalists pushing for a federal override of state decisions bear none of the costs of their favored policies. Examples such as *Smithfield* and *Harmon* illustrate the point. In each case, the tradeoffs are complicated, and there is no reason to believe that the state is not adequately protecting the environment. What would be gained by elevating the matter into a national problem, to be handled by EPA or by a federal court reacting to private litigation?

Another area where reform is important concerns junk science. This reform, again, primarily applies to rulemaking, but the quality of information used in enforcement must be maintained. In particular, the effort of the Credible Evidence Rule to formalize the agency's right to rely on anything it pleases should be resisted. On this issue, however, it is difficult to think of any productive action except litigation when EPA actually begins to enforce its new rule.

The Lost Art of Legal Self-Defense

One of the most important steps toward reform would be for industry to start defending itself more vigorously. A recent monograph titled "No Comment and Other Admissions of Guilt" laments the tendency of business to go into a shell when confronted with accusations, and contrasts that behavior with that of plaintiffs' lawyers and environmentalists who never meet a reporter or a microphone they do not love.[22] Certainly, in gathering information for this book, I have often found it difficult to get industry people to defend their positions on the record. When I complained about this to one lawyer, he commented that his clients really do fear agency retaliation if they protest too much against overreaching enforcement. Given the breadth and uncertainty discussed previously, a company knows full well that if agency officials get angry at some public statement and decide to retaliate, they will certainly be able to do so. In such circumstances, no one wants to risk public complaint.

In the longer term, this reticence gains little. EPA has a political need for a continuing supply of targets, preferably high-profile ones. Doing everything EPA demands is no guarantee that companies will not be sued for failing to anticipate what the agency might think at some point in the future. As the diesel engine manufacturers learned, it is not safe to assume that tacit or even explicit bargains with EPA will be kept.

At the very least, companies should release their own analyses of enforcement cases, explaining the situation from their point of view, and explaining what environmental harm was or was not involved. For example, the electric utilities, the pulp and paper industry, and the petroleum refiners all appeared at a Senate hearing on February 28, 2001, on the topic of New Source Review under the Clean Air Act. Although discussion was ostensibly limited to possible EPA rulemaking, the testimony could not avoid discussing the pending litigation against the utilities. The statements contain a lode of information on the issues, the history, the reasons companies have made the choices EPA is now attacking, and the problems that EPA is inflicting on the industries.[23]

This material is useful and important, but it received no press. Few people know of its existence. And it certainly was not available in November 1999, when EPA blasted the utilities with press releases portraying them as blatant violators of the law, a portrait that has gone uncontradicted. Similarly, the diesel engine manufacturers let their portrayal as villains pass unrebutted, and so did the automobile manufacturers.

Such passive behavior may not be irrational from the point of view of an individual company. I asked one corporate official about a particular issue, and he said, roughly, "Look, this was a one-day story, and we have no interest in making it into a multi-day story, so we are saying nothing. If it comes back, then maybe we will explain our position. But we do not think we can win in the press, so we regard silence as our best option."

From the point of view of the short-term interest of his company, he may well be right. But a collective-good problem is involved; namely, the continuing spate of unchallenged EPA press releases tars all of industry, furthers EPA's political agenda, and fosters a legal climate in which agency discretion and power go unchecked.

Industry in general could learn a valuable lesson from W.R. Grace, which was unfairly pilloried in the book and then the movie *A Civil Action.* As public relations expert Rose Marshall wrote,

> When the movie was about to be released, the company, recognizing that it had a problem, responded with considerable astuteness. It set up a Web site loaded with detailed factual information on the incident, its history, and its resolution [www.civil-action.com]. The site includes many of the documents relevant to the controversy, such as government reports and risk assessments, so that the viewer can see the raw material, unfiltered by either corporate PR people or plaintiffs' lawyers. Any reporter or citizen wanting information can find it quickly and easily.
>
> There is no way of knowing the overall impact of the company's effort, but it is indisputable that numerous stories appeared pointing out the problems with the Hollywood version of events, and that the movie's release did not trigger the kind of media feeding frenzy that has developed in other contexts. There is nothing like complex facts for discouraging simplistic treatment—but writers have to be able to find them.[24]

91

In the end, perhaps the course for reform is clear after all. People who believe in the rule of law as a principle, and those who believe in the rule of law because they have much to lose from its decline, must fight for it on every front: They should draft legislation, insist on congressional hearings, batter the courts with briefs, lobby the executive branch, and defend themselves in the media every time and in every context that the rule of law is challenged.

Notes

Introduction

1. See, for example, Joel A. Mintz, *Enforcement at the EPA: High Stakes and Hard Choices* (Austin: University of Texas Press, 1995).
2. F. A. Hayek, *The Road to Serfdom* (Chicago: University of Chicago Press, 1944, 1976), p. 72.
3. Robert Conquest, *Reflections on a Ravaged Century* (New York: W.W. Norton, 2000), p. 33.

Chapter 1

1. See, for example, Clifford Rechtschaffen, "Deterrence versus Cooperation and the Evolving Theory of Environmental Enforcement," *Southern California Law Review* 71, (1998); Glass Geltman and Andrew E. Skroback, "Reinventing the EPA to Conform with the New American Environmentality," *Columbia Journal of Environmental Law* 23, 1 (1998).
2. Indur M. Goklany, *Clearing the Air: The Real Story of the War on Air Pollution* (Washington: Cato Institute, 1999).
3. Bruce A. Ackerman, *Clean Coal/Dirty Air: Or How the Clean Air Act Became a Multibillion-Dollar Bail-Out for High-Sulfur Coal Producers and What Should Be Done about It* (New Haven: Yale University Press, 1981).
4. See Douglas C. Michael, "Cooperative Implementation of Federal Regulations," *Yale Journal of Regulation* 13, 535 (1996).
5. Telephone and E-mail interviews with Eleanor Lindway, owner of Precision Plating, June 28, 29, and 30, 2000.
6. David Armstrong, "U.S. Judge Rules EPA Harassed Mill Owner," *Boston Globe*, August 1, 2000, p. A1.
7. Gregory D. Page, "Counting Beans at the Environmental Protection Agency," *Environmental Law and Property Rights News*, Federalist Society, Fall 2000, p. 4.
8. All figures in this subsection come from EPA, *FY98 Accomplishments*, passim.
9. Ibid., p. 3. For a discussion of SEPs from a respondent's point of view, see Christopher D. Carey, "Negotiating Environmental Penalties: Guidance on the Use of Supplemental Environmental Projects," *Air Force Law Review* 44, 1 (1998). For an environmentalist argument against the use of SEPs, see David A. Dana, "The Uncertain Merits of Environmental Enforcement Reform: The Case of Supplemental Environmental Projects," *Wisconsin Law Review* 1181 (1998).
10. Daniel Riesel, *Environmental Enforcement: Civil and Criminal* (New York: Law Journal Press, 1997, with annual updates through 2000), § 7.03[1], pp. 7–44.
11. EPA Press Release, November 4, 1999, es.epa.gov/oeca/enforcement/dec99/nation.html.

12. EPA Press Release, "Man Ordered to Pay $4.74 Million for Failing to Clean Up Gasoline Leak That Contaminated Residential Drinking Water," June 1, 2000, www.usdoj.gov/opa/pr/2000/June/311enrd.htm.

13. Riesel, § 1.04[2], p. 1–13.

14. EPA, *FY98 Accomplishments*, p. 2.

15. Ibid.

16. Ibid.

17. "EPA/CMA Root Cause Analysis Pilot Project: An Industry Survey," 1999, http://es.epa.gov/oeca/ccsmd/rootcause. The Chemical Manufacturers Association is now named the American Chemistry Council.

18. Gregg Easterbrook, "Sunny Side Up," *New Republic*, June 19, 2000.

Chapter 2

1. Riesel, § 7.01[1], pp. 7–2, 7–3.

2. John F. Cooney et al., *Environmental Crimes Deskbook* (Washington: Environmental Law Institute, 1996), p. 12. Cited hereafter as *ELI Deskbook*.

3. Riesel, § 7.01[1], pp. 7–2, 7–3.

4. Earl J. Devaney, director, EPA Office of Criminal Enforcement, Memorandum to All EPA Employees Working in or in Support of the Criminal Enforcement Program, January 12, 1994, reprinted in *ELI Deskbook*, p. 111.

5. Riesel, § 7.01[1], pp. 7–3.

6. See, for example, Kevin A. Gaynor and Thomas R. Bartman, "Specific Intent Standard for Environmental Crimes: An Idea Whose Time Has Come," *Environment Reporter*, Bureau of National Affairs, March 10, 1995, pp. 2206, 2209–11.

7. *ELI Deskbook*, p. 9.

8. Leslie Spencer, "Designated Inmates," *Forbes*, October 26, 1992, p.100, quoted in Timothy Lynch, "Polluting Our Principles: Environmental Prosecutions and the Bill of Rights," Cato Institute Policy Analysis no. 223, April 20, 1995, p. 10.

9. Ibid.

10. Sheila Balkan, "Preparing the Business Client for Criminal Proceedings," ABA Section of Litigation, paper no. 531-0023/5H, November 1993.

11. *ELI Deskbook*, p. 9.

12. General Accounting Office, "Environmental Protection: More Consistency Needed among EPA Regions in Approach to Enforcement," GAO/RCED-00-108, June 2000.

13. Roger J. Marzulla, Testimony before the Subcommittee on Commercial and Administrative Law, Committee on the Judiciary, U.S. House of Representatives, Concerning H.R. 4049, Regulatory Fair Warning Act, May 7, 1998, www.house.gov/judiciary/5407.htm.

14. Environmental Law Institute, "Barriers to Environmental Technology Innovation and Use," 1998. See also ELI, "Innovation, Cost and Regulation: Perspectives on Business, Policy and Legal Factors Affecting the Cost of Environmental Compliance," 1999.

15. Marzulla.

Chapter 3

1. *United States v. International Minerals and Chemical Co.*, 438 U.S. 422 (1971).

2. In *United States v. Staples*, 114 S. Ct. 1793 (1994), the Court ruled that the government must show that a defendant knew the weapon was a machine gun. It was not

enough to prove only that he possessed it, or that he knew it was dangerous, or that he knew that some guns are subject to regulation. He had to know of the characteristics that made it a machine gun. In *Ratzlaf v.United States*, 114 S. Ct. 655 (1994), the Court ruled that a defendant must know that structuring cash withdrawals so as to avoid requirements that withdrawals of more than $10,000 be reported was illegal. In *Posters 'N' Things v. United States*, 114 S. Ct. 1793 (1994), the Court ruled that a defendant must know that items sold were likely to be used with illegal drugs and that he was using an interstate conveyance. In *United States v. X-Citement Video*, 114 S. Ct. 1464 (1994), the Court ruled that a defendant must know that the performer in a sexually explicit videotape was a minor.

3. See Richard J. Lazarus, "Meeting the Demands of Integration in the Evolution of Environmental Law: Reforming Environmental Criminal Law," 83 *Georgetown Law Journal* 2407, 2468–84 (1995). See also Riesel, § 6.03, pp. 6–42, 6–66.

4. 101 F.3d 386 (5th Cir. 1996).

5. 1 F.3d 1523, *amended on denial of rehearing and rehearing en banc*, 35 F.3d 1275 (9th Cir. 1994), *cert. denied*, 115 S. Ct. 939, 1995.

6. Richard J. Lazarus, "Meeting the Demands of Integration in the Evolution of Environmental Law: Reforming Environmental Criminal Law," 83 *Georgetown Law Journal* 2407, 2476–84 (1995). The Court also retreated from its 1994 decisions in *Bryan v. United States*, 118 S. Ct. 1939 (1998). In *Bryan*, the statute said that a violation must be "willful," which is usually regarded as a signal that Congress meant to require actual awareness of the law. The Court upheld a conviction when the defendant knew he was dealing in firearms and knew his conduct was illegal under state law but did not necessarily know that he was violating a *federal* law. It distinguished *Ratzlaf* and the tax cases, in which "willful" *is* interpreted as requiring actual knowledge of the law, as "involving highly technical statutes that present the danger of ensnaring individuals engaged in apparently innocent conduct. As a result, we held that these statutes 'carve out an exception to the traditional rule' that ignorance of the law is no excuse."

7. 53 F.3d 533, 542 (2d Cir.), *cert. denied*, 116 S. Ct. 773 (1995).

8. 167 F.3d 1176 (7th Cir. 1999).

9. Adding to the negative side of the opinion in *Kelly* are a series of judicial statements to the effect that Congress defined hazardous waste, so once Kelly knew the substance had a potential to do harm, he was on notice to find out its status. In fact, the congressional definitions are vague, and EPA's gloss on them is far from clear. In particular, the question of whether gasoline, one substance involved in *Kelly*, can be hazardous waste is a knotty issue, and federal courts have split on it. The judge writing the opinion in the case did not demonstrate any knowledge of this controversy.

10. 176 F.3d 1116 (9th Cir., 1999), *cert. denied*, 120 S. Ct. 860 (2000).

11. EPA, "Enforcement and Compliance Assurance Accomplishments Report, FY 1997," EPA-300-R-98-003, July 1998.

12. EPA, "Enforcement and Compliance Assurance Accomplishments Report, FY 1996," May 1997, p. B-81, es.epa.gov/oeca/96accomp/96accomp.pdf.

13. Pacific and Arctic Pipelines was convicted of making false statements to the U.S. Coast Guard investigators. The report does not say whether this conviction followed a trial or resulted from a plea. Ibid.

14. EPA, Press Release, "U.S. Settles Environmental Claims with Union Pacific Railroad: Train Derailments in Utah and Colorado Led to Fuel Spills," June 8, 2000, p. 2.

15. *Statistical Abstract of the United States*, 119th ed., 1999, Table 402.

16. EPA, Press Release, "U.S. Settles Environmental Claims with Union Pacific Railroad: Train Derailments in Utah and Colorado Led to Fuel Spills."

17. Justices Thomas and O'Connor dissented from the denial of certiorari on the ground that the courts of appeals are invoking the "narrow" public welfare doctrine too readily, and that the Supreme Court needs "to further delineate its limits." *Hanousek v. United States*, 120 S. Ct. 860 (2000) (Thomas, J., dissenting from the denial of certiorari).

18. David Stirling, "Most Favored Error Designation," *Washington Times*, May 28, 2000, B1.

Chapter 4

1. 5 U.S.C. § 552 says that a person cannot be affected by substantive rules or interpretations of general applicability unless he had actual and timely notice of their terms. However, this has been treated as a requirement that rules be published, not that they be intelligible or widely disseminated. Also, it has never been held to apply to interpretations made in the course of litigation.

2. *Tenneco Oil Co. v. Federal Energy Admin.*, 613 F.2d 298, 303 (Temp. Emer. Ct. App. 1980).

3. 411 U.S. 655 (1973).

4. 53 F.3d 1324 (D.C. Cir. 1995).

5. 158 F.3d 1350 (D.C. Cir. 1998).

6. *United States v. Hoechst-Celanese Corp.*, 128 F.3d 216 (4th Cir. 1997), *cert. denied*, 118 S. Ct. 2367 (1998).

7. 128 F.3d at 230, 233. If this case were decided today, this dissent should prevail on the basis of *Christensen v. Harris County*, 120 S. Ct. 1655 (2000).

8. See James V. DeLong, *Property Matters: How Property Rights Are under Assault— And Why You Should Care* (New York: Free Press, 1997), pp. 91–152. The practice of retaliating against those who challenge agency interpretations of the law is apparent in the enforcement of wetlands restrictions, which is shared by EPA and the Army Corps of Engineers. The people prosecuted are those who, when informed of the particular theory under which the government regards their property as wetland (and there are many of these theories, and they by no means require that the ground actually be wet), react by saying "that's ridiculous!" and then proceed to use their property as they see fit. The government responds to such acts of lese majesty by bringing a criminal action instead of a civil action that would allow the substantive issue to be resolved in an orderly manner.

9. Andrew Fois, assistant attorney general, Office of Legislative Affairs, U.S. Dept. of Justice, Letter to Charles T. Canady, chairman, Subcommittee on the Constitution, House Committee on the Judiciary, September 20, 1995.

10. Statement of Joseph N. Onek, deputy associate attorney general, Hearings on the Regulatory Fair Warning Act (H.R. 4049), Subcommittee on Commercial and Administrative Law, House Judiciary Committee, July 23, 1998, www.house.gov/judiciary/5411.htm.

11. Statement of Chairman George W. Gekas (R-Pa.), Hearings on the Regulatory Fair Warning Act (H.R. 881), Subcommittee on Commercial and Administrative Law, House Judiciary Committee, June 29, 1999, www.house.gov/judiciary/geka0629.htm.

Chapter 5

1. See, for example, *Syncor Int'l Corp. v. Shalala*, 127 F.3d 90 (1997).

2. EPA, Office of Regulatory Enforcement, Press Release on coal-fired power plants enforcement, November 3, 1999, es.epa.gov/oeca/ore/aed/coal/index.html. This Web site links to other EPA documents in the case, such as the Notices of Violation, Complaints, and Speeches.

3. EPA Press Release, "U.S. Expands Clean Air Act Lawsuits against Electric Utilities," March 1, 2000. EPA recently revamped its Web site, and many old press releases are no longer retrievable, including this one.

4. EPA Press Release, "U.S. Settles Landmark Clean Air Act Case against Electric Utility," February 29, 2000. EPA recently revamped its Web site, and many old press releases are no longer retrievable, including this one.

5. "Utility Settles Lawsuit for $1.4 Billion," *Washington Post*, December 22, 2000, p. A5.

6. Tom Kenworthy, "Broad EPA Probes Target Refineries," *Washington Post*, November 11, 1999, p. A12. See also Hearings before the Subcommittee on Clean Air, Wetlands, Private Property and Nuclear Safety, Senate Committee on Environment and Public Works, Concerning the New Source Review Regulatory Program, Cincinnati, Ohio, February 28, 2000, passim, www.senate.gov/~epw/sla_0228.htm. Cited hereafter as *NSR Hearings*.

7. The author attended the argument, and this is his recollection. The quote is not exact.

8. *Chevron U.S.A. v. Natural Resources Defense Council*, 467 U.S. 837, 851 (1984).

9. Comprehensive Environmental Response, Compensation, and Liability Act, 42 U.S.C. § 9601(14)(F).

10. See Regulatory Impact Analysis, Inc, "Choices in Risk Assessment: The Role of Science Policy in the Environmental Risk Assessment Process," report prepared for Sandia National Laboratories: Washington, D.C., 1994.

11. Statement of John Seitz, director, EPA Office of Air Quality Planning and Standards, *NSR Hearings*.

12. See, for example Frank P. Grad, *Treatise on Environmental Law* (New York: Matthew Bender, 1973), vol. 1, sec. 2.01-2.04, pp. 2–1 to 2–555.

13. Statement of David Hawkins, director, Air and Energy Programs, Natural Resources Defense Council, *NSR Hearings*.

14. Statement of W. Henson Moore, president and CEO, American Forest and Paper Association, *NSR Hearings*.

15. Statement of Moore; Statement of John S. Seitz.

16. Statement of Moore.

17. "*Recently*, two senior EPA staff members heavily involved in the NSR reform discussions publicly debated the 'correct' interpretation of its 'actual to potential' NSR policy. If EPA officials can't figure it out and agree on a single meaning, how are states and industry supposed to?" Ibid.

18. Statement of Bill Tyndall, vice president of environmental services, Cinergy Corp., *NSR Hearing*.

19. Statement of Joe Bynum, executive vice president, TVA, *NSR Hearings*.

20. See Motion of Petitioner Tennessee Valley Authority for Stay of Agency Order, in *TVA v. EPA*, Dkt. No. 00-12310-E, 11th Cir., filed May 16, 2000; American Petroleum Institute and National Petrochemical and Refiners Association, "New Source Performance Standards (NSPS) Subpart J Applicability and Compliance Determination

Issues," submission to the EPA National Task Force Reviewing the Applicability of NSPSs for Petroleum Refineries, February 26, 1999.

21. Julie R. Domike and Alec Zacaroli, "EPA's Reinterpretation of NSR Regulations Could Have Costly Implications for Businesses," *Environmental Reporter*, Bureau of National Affairs, March 3, 2000, pp. 407–11.

22. Ibid.

23. TVA, Motion for Stay, p. 25.

24. "High Gas Prices? Blame EPA," *Investor's Business Daily*, June 14, 2000.

25. NEPDG, "Reliable, Affordable, and Environmentally Sound Energy for America's Future," May 2001, www.whitehouse.gov/energy. On June 22, 2001, EPA released a background paper on the NSR program and announced a schedule of public meetings. This material is available at www.epa.gov/air/nsr-review.

26. See EPA Press Release, "U.S. Reaches Clean Air Settlement with Petroleum Refiner," July 12, 2001.

27. In addition to the cases examined closely in this section, General Motors was charged with putting on "illegal devices" to defeat pollution controls that resulted in emissions of carbon monoxide (CO) that were thrice the legal limit. In 1995, GM paid an $11 million penalty, spent $25 million to recall 500,000 vehicles, and funded $7 million in SEPs. EPA, "Enforcement and Compliance Assurance Accomplishments Report, FY 1996," p. B-72. Even if GM took the action alleged (and the truth is not clear), CO pollution is a problem in the winter, not in the summer. Yet this particular case was filed because GM equipped Cadillacs with a device that allowed increased emissions of CO when the air conditioner was on. Because this event does not occur in the winter, the environmental harm caused by the device was zero. Jonathan H. Adler, "Bean Counting for a Better Earth: Environmental Enforcement at the EPA," *Regulation*, Spring 1998, pp. 40, 47. Therefore, EPA's public relations focused on *potential* health effects, even though former EPA administrator Carol Browner lashed the company for "sacrificing the public health" and "defying the laws." Ibid.

EPA said that Honda "disabled the misfire monitoring devices" on 1.6 million cars. In June 1998, Honda settled with the agency. Honda was required to extend emissions warranties and provide some free maintenance. The cost was estimated at $250 million. At the same time, Ford was accused of attaching a device to enhance fuel economy that increased fuel mileage at high speeds but had the unanticipated effect of increasing nitrogen oxide emissions. For this crime, Ford was forced in June 1998 to recall 60,000 vans, pay $2.5 million in civil penalties, and buy 2,500 tons of nitrogen oxide credits for $2.5 million. EPA, "Enforcement Alert," August 1998.

28. DOJ Press Release, "Mazda Motor of America to Settle Clean Air Act Case," September 30, 1999.

29. Complaint, *United States of America v. Toyota Motor Sales U.S.A.* (D.D.C., Filed July 12, 1999), No. 1:99CV01888. Hereafter cited as Federal Complaint.

30. DOJ Press Release, "U.S. Sues Toyota for Clean Air Act Violations; Claims 2.2 Million Cars Have Illegal Emission Control Monitoring Systems," July 12, 1999, www.usdoj.gov/opa/pr/1999/July/298enr.htm.

31. California EPA News Release, "ARB Orders Repair Plan for 330,000 Toyota and Lexus Autos," September 2, 1998.

32. Joseph B. White and Gregory L. White, "California Regulators Seek Court Order for Toyota Recall over Pollution Sensor," *Wall Street Journal*, December 14, 1998, p. B3; off-the-record conversations with people involved in the case.

33. Toyota Press Release, "Toyota Reaffirms Its Position on Emissions Situation," January 8, 1999.

34. Federal Complaint.

35. Holman W. Jenkins Jr., "Who Controls the Idiot Light?" *Wall Street Journal*, July 21, 1999, p. A23.

36. Carol M. Browner, Remarks prepared for delivery at announcement of settlement with heavy duty diesel manufacturers, October 22, 1998.

37. EPA, "Proposed Rule on Control of Air Pollution from New Motor Vehicles and Motor Vehicle Engines," 44 *Federal Register* 9464 (February 13, 1979).

38. House Committee on Commerce, "Asleep at the Wheel: The Environmental Protection Agency's Failure to Enforce Pollution Standards for Heavy-Duty Diesel Trucks," staff report, March 2000, www.house.gov/commerce/asleepatthewheel-htm.html. Hereafter cited as "Asleep at the Wheel." Page numbers refer to a printout of an Internet download made on April 6, 2000.

39. Commission on Geosciences, Environment and Resources, National Academy of Sciences, *Rethinking the Ozone Problem in Urban and Regional Air Pollution* (Washington: National Academy Press, 1992). EPA has a chart showing thousands of premature deaths from NO. "Asleep at the Wheel," p. 14. Like most EPA risk assessments, this is dubious. See Michael Gough and Steven Milloy, "EPA's Cancer Risk Guidelines: Guidance to Nowhere," Cato Institute Policy Analysis no. 263, November 12, 1996.

40. Jim Gilligan, "'EPA Betrayed Us': Engine Makers Say Agency Knew about Test," *Transport Topics*, November 2, 1998; John G. Parker, "EPA Knew Its Engine Tests Were Flawed, Volvo Says," *Transport Topics*, November 23, 1998; John Parker and Jeff Johnson, "Evidence Grows that EPA Knew about Test Flaws," *Transport Topics*, December 21, 1998.

41. Jeff Johnson, "EPA Refutes Engine Makers' Claims," *Transport Topics*, December 21, 1998.

42. "Asleep at the Wheel."

43. Julie DeFalco, "The Deadly Effects of Fuel Economy Standards: CAFE's Lethal Impact on Auto Safety," Competitive Enterprise Institute, June 1, 1999. This analysis cites a plethora of support for its conclusions about the death toll exacted by CAFE, including the U.S. Court of Appeals for the D.C. Circuit. See *CEI and Consumer Alert v. NHTSA*, 956 F.2d 321 (D.C. Cir. 1992); *CEI and Consumer Alert v. NHTSA*, 45 F.3d 481 (D.C. Cir. 1995).

44. Jeff Johnson, "Interim Step in EPA Engine Pact," *Transport Topics*, November 25, 1998; "Asleep at the Wheel," p. 12; off-the-record conversations with parties familiar with the negotiations.

45. Mike Osenga, "EPA v. Diesel: Diesel Industry Confronts the Emissions Settlement," *Diesel Progress*, December 1998, www.dieselpub.com/events/epa_issue.htm.

Chapter 6

1. EPA, "Credible Evidence Revisions," 62 *Federal Register* 8314 (February 24, 1997).

2. *Clean Air Implementation Project v. EPA*, 150 F.3d 1200, 1204 (D.C. Cir. 1998).

3. Interviews with various participants.

4. Comments of Robert Ajax, in EPA, Transcript of Credible Evidence Stakeholders Meeting, April 2, 1996, pp. 107–23. Cited hereafter as Stakeholders Meeting.

5. Ibid., p. 120.

6. Michael H. Levin, "EPA's Indefensible 'Credible Evidence' Rule: A Critical Analysis," Washington Legal Foundation, May 1997.

7. EPA, Clean Air Act Credible Evidence Final Rule, 62 *Federal Register* 8313 (February 24, 1997).

8. Comments of Rob Brubaker, Stakeholders Meeting, p. 60.

9. Riesel, § 4.02[1], p. 4–11.

10. Comments of John Medley, Stakeholders Meeting, p. 33.

11. EPA, "Compliance Assurance Monitoring," 62 *Federal Register* 54899 (October 22, 1997).

12. EPA, *In the Matter of City of Salisbury, Maryland*, Dkt No. CWI-III, Order Granting in Part and Denying in Part Complainant's Motion for Accelerated Decision, www.epa.gov/aljhomep/orders/salisbur.htm.

Chapter 7

1. See, for example, David Schoenbrod, *Power without Responsibility: How Congress Abuses the People through Delegation* (New Haven: Yale University Press, 1993).

2. 33 U.S.C. § 411.

3. See, for example, *United States v. Pennsylvania Chemical Co.*, 411 U.S. 655 (1973).

4. 33 U.S.C. §§ 1251–1387.

5. For an excellent review of the topic, see Jonathan H. Adler, "Wetlands, Waterfowl, and the Menace of Mr. Wilson: Commerce Clause Jurisprudence and the Limits of Federal Wetlands Regulation," *Environmental Law* 29, 1 (1999).

6. *United States v. Wilson*, 133 F.3d 251 (4th Circuit 1997).

7. *Solid Waste Agency of Northern Cook County v. U.S. Army Corps of Engineers*, S. Ct. (2001).

8. U.S. Army Corps of Engineers and Environmental Protection Agency, Final Rule on Excavation, 58 *Federal Register* 45008 (August 25, 1993).

9. *National Mining Association v. U.S. Army Corps of Engineers*, 145 F.3rd 1401 (D.C. Cir. 1998).

10. *In re Slinger Drainage, Inc.*, EPA Board of Environmental Appeals, Dkt. No. 5-CWA-97-022, CWA Appeal No. 98-10, September 29, 1999.

11. See Jane F. Barrett and Jeanne M. Grasso, "Development of Environmental Criminal Enforcement and Its Impact on the Maritime Industry," Paper presented at MarineLog, Program on Tanker and Maritime Legislation 98, September 22–23, 1998.

12. Daniel J. Murphy, "EPA's Highway to Traffic Hell?" *Investor's Business Daily*, April 2, 1999.

13. Peter Samuel and Randal O'Toole, "Smart Growth at the Federal Trough: EPA's Financing of the Anti-Sprawl Movement," Cato Institute Policy Analysis no. 361, November 24, 1999, pp. 4–5.

14. Christopher H. Foreman Jr., *The Promise and Peril of Environmental Justice* (Washington: Brookings Institution, 1998); Michael Steinberg, "Making Sense of Environmental Justice," National Legal Center for the Public Interest, June 1999.

15. Michael Gough, "Biotech—Boom or Bust," *CEI Update*, April 1999, p. 3.

Chapter 8

1. Testimony by Becky Norton Dunlop, secretary of natural resources, Commonwealth of Virginia, before the Senate Committee on Environment and Public Works, Hearings on the Relationship between the Federal and State Governments in the

Enforcement of Environmental Laws, June 10, 1997, www.senate.gov/~epw/stmt_105.htm#6_10_97. Cited hereafter as Dunlop Statement.

2. Alexis de Tocqueville Institution.

3. Dunlop Statement; Goklany.

4. *U.S. v. Smithfield Foods, Inc.*, 191 F.3rd 516 (4th Cir. 1999), *cert. denied*, 531 U.S. 813 (2000).

5. Statement of Lois J. Shiffer, assistant attorney general for natural resources, U.S. DOJ, before the Senate Committee on Environment and Public Works, Hearings on the Relationship between the Federal and State Governments in the Enforcement of Environmental Laws, June 10, 1997, www.senate.gov/~epw/stmt_105.htm#6_10_97. Cited hereafter as Schiffer Statement.

6. Ibid.

7. Dunlop Statement.

8. Ibid. Goklany, pp. 83–95. See also David Ridenour, "Politics Painted Green: EPA Uses Enforcement as Partisan Political Weapon," Policy Analysis no. 213, National Center for Public Policy Research, September 1998.

9. *Harmon Industries v. Browner*, 191 F.3d 894 (8th Cir. 1999), *affirming, Harmon Industries v. Browner*, 19 F. Supp. 988 (W.D. Mo. 1998). EPA chose not to seek *certiorari*. The facts are recounted in the two opinions, and in material prepared for a bar association conference by one of Harmon's lawyers. Terry Satterlee, "Caught in the Crossfire: Industry Perspective on State/EPA Enforcement," ABA Section of Natural Resources, Energy, and Environmental Law, 28th Annual Conference on Environmental Law, Keystone, Colo., March 11–14, 1999.

10. Statement of Robert E. Harmon, chairman, Harmon Industries, before the Senate Committee on Environment and Public Works, Hearings on the Relationship between the Federal and State Governments in the Enforcement of Environmental Laws, June 10, 1997, www.senate.gov/~epw/stmt_105.htm#6_10_97.

11. The court's statement of facts is not clear on what this means. Apparently, Harmon and MDNR chose to treat the contamination site as a formal "hazardous waste disposal site" and then discontinue its use under the closure provisions of RCRA, which require continuing monitoring and provision for financial responsibility.

12. Satterlee.

13. EPA, "Incentives for Self-Policing: Discovery, Disclosure, Correction and Prevention of Violations," 60 *Federal Register* 66,706 (December 22, 1995); EPA, "Final Policy Statement on Incentives for Self-Policing: Discovery, Disclosure, Correction and Prevention of Violations," 64 *Federal Register* 19,617 (April 11, 2000).

14. Barry M. Harman, Leif B. King, and John J. McDonald, "Environmental Audits: How Uncooperative Federalism Undermines Environmental Protection," National Legal Center for the Public Interest, August 1998, pp. 1–2.

15. Adler, "Bean Counting for a Better Earth: Environmental Enforcement at the EPA," pp. 40, 45–46.

16. EPA, Final Policy Statement on Incentives for Self-Policing: Discovery, Disclosure, Correction and Prevention of Violations, 64 *Federal Register* 19,617 (April 11, 2000). The conditions are systematic discovery through an environmental audit or compliance management system, voluntary discovery, prompt disclosure, discovery and disclosure independent of government or third-party plaintiff, correction and remediation, prevent recurrence, no repeat violations, other violations excluded, and cooperation.

17. www.newenvironmentalism.org.

Chapter 9

1. Lynch.
2. David Lyons, "Attorneys Say Gov't Prosecutors Stepping on Toes," *Law News Network*, September 10, 1999; Maud Mater, chair of board, American Corporate Counsel Association, Letter to Eric Holder, deputy attorney general, May 12, 2000, www.acca.com/gcadvocate/advocacy/holder.html; Andrea Foster, "GCs Protest Prosecutor Tactics," *National Law Journal*, May 29, 2000, p. B1.
3. Harvey A. Silvergate and Andrew Good, "Starr Teachers," *Reason*, May 1999, p. 26.
4. *United States v. Omega Chemical Corp.*, 153 F.3d 994 (9th Cir. 1998).

Chapter 10

1. See, for example, Kevin A. Gaynor, "A System Spinning Out of Control," *Environmental Forum*, May–June 1990, p. 28.
2. Fred L. Smith Jr., "Conclusion: Environmental Policy at the Crossroads," in Michaei S. Greve and Fred J. Smith Jr. eds., *Environmental Politics: Public Costs, Private Rewards* (New York: Praeger, 1992), pp. 177, 183.
3. See, for example, James V. DeLong, "Informal Rulemaking and the Integration of Law and Policy," *Virginia Law Review* 65, 257 (1979), and James V. DeLong, "New Wine for a New Bottle: Judicial Review in the Regulatory State," *Virginia Law Review* 72, 399 (1986), both of which discuss EPA's problems in the 1970s, particularly the difficulties caused by its character as a "single-mission" agency devoted to the environment, and resistant of tradeoffs with other values.
4. Sidney Shapiro, "Political Oversight and the Deterioration of Regulatory Policy," *Administrative Law Review* 46, 1 (1994). Provisions enacted include the Paperwork Reduction Act of 1995; the Unfunded Mandates Reform Act of 1995; the Small Business Enforcement Fairness Act of 1996; Executive Order 12612 (1987) on Federalism Impact; Executive Orders 12912 and 12498, both superseded by Executive Order 12866; and Executive Order 12630, Government Actions and Interference with Constitutionally Protected Property Rights (March 15, 1988).
5. GAO, "Federalism: Implementation of Executive Order 12612 in the Rulemaking Process," T/GGD-99-93, May 5, 1999, p. 5. Other agencies were no better; of 11,414 rules issued by nonindependent regulatory agencies during this period, exactly 5 were accompanied by federalism impact analyses.
6. W. Michael McCabe, acting deputy administrator, EPA, Letter to the National Association of Manufacturers, Washington, D.C., June 22, 2000, www.epa.gov/epahome/speeches_0622.htm. For earlier critiques of EPA's overall philosophy and approach, see, for example, EPA, Science Advisory Board, "Reducing Risk: Setting Priorities and Strategies for Environmental Protection," SAB-EC-90-021, September 1990; Marc K. Landy, Marc J. Roberts, and Stephen R. Thomas, *The Environmental Protection Agency: Asking the Wrong Questions* (New York: Oxford University Press, 1989).
7. See, for example, EPA, Office of Policy Analysis, "Unfinished Business: A Comparative Assessment of Environmental Problems: Overview Report," February 1987.
8. The term was coined by Professor Richard Stewart, in "The Reformation of American Administrative Law," *Harvard Law Review* 88, 1667 (1975).

9. A rich literature on "public choice" exists. See, for example, Fred S. McChesney, *Money for Nothing* (Cambridge: Harvard University Press, 1997); George J. Stigler, ed., *Chicago Studies in Political Economy* (Chicago: University of Chicago Press, 1988).

10. For more detailed discussion of this point, see James V. DeLong, "New Wine for a New Bottle."

11. *Volkswagenwerk Aktiengesellschaft v. Federal Maritime Commission*, 390 U.S. 261, 273 (1968).

12. 467 U.S. 837 (1984).

13. *Bowles v. Seminole Rock Sand and Gravel Co.*, 325 U.S. 410, 414 (1945).

14. John F. Manning, "Constitutional Structure and Judicial Deference to Agency Interpretations of Agency Rules," *Columbia Law Review* 96, 612, 617 (1996).

15. Statement of Daniel E. Troy, Hearings on the Regulatory Fair Warning Act (H.R. 4049), Subcommittee on Commercial and Administrative Law, House Judiciary Committee, July 23, 1998, www.house.gov/judiciary/5412.htm. The quotation in Troy's statement is from Manning, p. 660. The internal quote within the quotation from Manning is cited to Max Radin, "Statutory Interpretation," *Harvard Law Review* 43, 863, 884 (1930).

16. *Sutton v. United Airlines*, 119 S. Ct. 2139 (1999).

17. Ibid.

18. *FDA v. Brown and Williamson Tobacco Co.*, 120 S. Ct. 12910 (2000).

19. See, for example, *Chicago v. Environmental Defense Fund*, 511 U.S. 328 (1994).

20. *Christensen v. Harris County*, 120 U.S. 1655 (May 1, 2000). A year earlier, in *Sutton v. United Airlines*, 119 U.S. 1655 (June 1999), the Court signaled concerns about *Chevron*. In a case on the Americans with Disabilities Act, it determined that the meaning of the statute was plain on its face, and therefore the interpretations of executive agencies would not be deferred to. The plain meaning discovered by the Supreme Court had escaped the notice of eight U.S. courts of appeal and three agencies, all of which had decided the issue the opposite of the way the Court did. *Sutton* also illustrates the fundamental problem with the assumption underlying *Chevron* that agencies are neutral interpreters of congressional will. The Equal Employment Opportunity Commission was trying to "interpret" the law in a way meant to add to the rolls of people classified as "disabled" everyone who wears eyeglasses, a move designed to increase the agency's clientele by a factor of two or three. The idea that an agency should receive deference in determining the scope of its own empire is hard to defend intellectually.

21. Justice David Souter, on the other hand, joined the majority only on the understanding that the interpretation *did* constitute a reasonable reading of the statute if the secretary of labor chose to issue a rule embodying it.

22. Rose Marshall, "No Comment and Other Confessions of Guilt," National Legal Center for the Public Interest, February 2000.

23. New Source Review Hearings, February 28, 2001.

24. Marshall, p. 20. For a review of the merits of the controversy, see James V. DeLong, "A Civil Action or a Civil Fiction: Hollywood Instructs America on Pollution and Greed," Competitive Enterprise Institute, January 1, 1999.

Index

107

About the Author

James V. DeLong is a senior fellow in the Project on Technology and Innovation at the Competitive Enterprise Institute in Washington, D.C.

Mr. DeLong writes often for scholarly, professional, and popular publications. His most recent book was *Property Matters: How Property Rights are Under Assault—And Why You Should Care*, published by Free Press in 1997. He has also published numerous articles in such outlets as the *Wall Street Journal*, the *Washington Times*, *Intellectual Capital*, the *New York Times*, the *National Law Journal*, the *New Republic*, the *Salt Lake Tribune*, *National Review Online*, and *TechCentralStation*.

He is a magna cum laude graduate of Harvard Law School, where he was book review editor of the *Harvard Law Review* and a cum laude graduate of Harvard College. He is a member of the bars of the District of Columbia, the State of California, and the Supreme Court of the United States and has served on the Committee on Scholarship of the Administrative Law Section of the American Bar Association.

Cato Institute

Founded in 1977, the Cato Institute is a public policy research foundation dedicated to broadening the parameters of policy debate to allow consideration of more options that are consistent with the traditional American principles of limited government, individual liberty, and peace. To that end, the Institute strives to achieve greater involvement of the intelligent, concerned lay public in questions of policy and the proper role of government.

The Institute is named for *Cato's Letters*, libertarian pamphlets that were widely read in the American Colonies in the early 18th century and played a major role in laying the philosophical foundation for the American Revolution.

Despite the achievement of the nation's Founders, today virtually no aspect of life is free from government encroachment. A pervasive intolerance for individual rights is shown by government's arbitrary intrusions into private economic transactions and its disregard for civil liberties.

To counter that trend, the Cato Institute undertakes an extensive publications program that addresses the complete spectrum of policy issues. Books, monographs, and shorter studies are commissioned to examine the federal budget, Social Security, regulation, military spending, international trade, and myriad other issues. Major policy conferences are held throughout the year, from which papers are published thrice yearly in the *Cato Journal*. The Institute also publishes the quarterly magazine *Regulation*.

In order to maintain its independence, the Cato Institute accepts no government funding. Contributions are received from foundations, corporations, and individuals, and other revenue is generated from the sale of publications. The Institute is a nonprofit, tax-exempt, educational foundation under Section 501(c)3 of the Internal Revenue Code.

CATO INSTITUTE
1000 Massachusetts Ave., N.W.
Washington, D.C. 20001